THE GLORY
WITHIN
YOU

THE GLORY
WITHIN
YOU

Modern Man and the Spirit

by
DUNCAN E. LITTLEFAIR

THE WESTMINSTER PRESS

PHILADELPHIA

Scripture quotations from the Revised Standard Version of the Bible are copyright, 1946 and 1952, by the
Division of Christian Education of the National Coun-
cil of Churches, and are used by permission.

Book design by Dorothy Alden Smith

Published by The Westminster Press®
Philadelphia, Pennsylvania

PRINTED IN THE UNITED STATES OF AMERICA

Library of Congress Cataloging in Publication Data

Littlefair, Duncan Elliot, 1912–
    The glory within you.

    Includes bibliographical references.
    1. Spirituality.   I. Title.
BV4501.2.L56   233   72–8972
ISBN 0–664–20960–2

Contents

Part III

IDENTITY
AND MORALITY

Part IV

SPIRITUAL
LEADERSHIP

Preface

The spirit is not some *thing*. It is not an identifiable object. It has no independent life of its own. The spirit is not something that can be separated from the body which gives it birth and through which it expresses itself. The spirit cannot be separated from the body or saved from the body or the world. The spirit is qualitative, it is an aspect of the world, it is an expression of the physical. Its glory is not to save itself from the world or the body, but rather to redeem the body and the world. The spirit illumines the world, lights up the darkness of mere matter. The spirit gives meaning, purpose, dignity, and worth to otherwise senseless or animal existence. The spirit is that which makes life human and "saves" human life. The spirit is the reason for religion and the basis of all religions, but it is not something apart from the world.

Christianity has fallen into the grave error of identifying the spirit as something that could be rescued from the world. In both professional religious thought and common practice it has been assumed that the only legitimate function of religion is to save the spirit from the world for a rich, full life where physical existence could not intrude, harass, or cripple it. In this traditional Christian view the world is a vale of tears and woe brought upon the spirit by its sinful association with unredeemable matter. The world of nature is a testing ground. If the tests are adequately met, the spirit will be rewarded by release from its painful worldly bondage to a life of bliss in some kind of heavenly realm.

This kind of dualism of body and spirit, nature and supernature, is no longer acceptable to the modern mind. For this reason our time is frequently designated as the post-Christian era. No matter what name is given to it or how it is described, it is clear that Christianity as we have known it is no longer vital and meaningful enough to direct our lives, command our attention, or inspire our hopes and ideals. We can no longer accept a religion designed by or created in a bilevel world. We need a religion that will help us find meaning, purpose, and direction within the natural world. We need a religion that will not try to help men escape from matter and time, but rather that will help find the glory within them. In the religion needed for this kind of world the spirit will not renounce the world or the flesh which gives it birth, but will welcome all the entanglements of sex, marriage, children, society, war, crime, business, education, labor, leisure, race, and ecology as an opportunity to express itself and thereby give all this swirling maelstrom of activity significance and worth.

This book is a simple attempt to participate in the creation of an adequate new religion by exploring the identity of the spirit. It should be understood at the outset that any term that has such a long and honored ancestry as the term "spirit" must be referring to something deeply vital and significant for human life regardless of how mistaken our understanding of it may have been. It should also be understood that if there is something that can be called spirit, it will be a natural part of our common daily human existence. It will not be something hidden, occult, or mysterious, but something so common, so pervasive, that we don't even notice it or think about it. "You have eyes but you see not, ears but you hear not."

If there is a failure in our life and religion, it is due to our having been looking for the wrong thing in the wrong place and missing the glory that was all about us waiting to be revealed by the light of our understanding—the light of the spirit. "Earth's a hard place in which to save the soul," but it is the only place we have. It is here in this troubled and troublesome world that the spirit must be found and saved.

This book is addressed to inquiring minds, to men and women of all ages and faiths who seek richer, more satisfying lives. I have tried to put the ideas in direct, everyday terms and to use simple illustrations. A good test of a religious concept is whether it makes sense when expressed in such terms.

I wish to acknowledge an unpayable debt to Henry Nelson Wieman, who re-naturalized religion for our day; Philip W. Buchen, who insisted that this book should be written; and David W. Ewing, who edited the transcripts and other basic materials used, saw the book through production, and offered valuable counsel at many stages. In addition, I am grateful to Alice McDowell for typing countless pages of manuscript and outline, and to Marian Kirchner for typing several late chapters and handling other work.

D. E. L.

Grand Rapids, Michigan

Part I

THE PARADOX
OF ACHIEVEMENT

Everyone His Own Hero

A new idea has begun to rule America. The idea is not new in men's minds and imaginations, but never before has it become reality. Now it is being realized—most conspicuously in the United States and other nations of the West, but also in the Soviet Union, Africa, Japan, and other areas. The result is a totally new trend in the history of man. I believe it will overshadow other current trends and developments, such as automation, urbanization, innovations in transportation, and shifts in the balance of power. It will overshadow the great leaders of our times. Beside it, other current history-making forces may someday seem quite insignificant.

This is the idea that no group or authority has a special claim to understanding, power, or influence. Every individual, however simple and common he may be, is entitled to find the meaning of life in and through himself. Direction properly comes from within the individual, within the group, not from over, above, or outside it.

Since the dawn of civilization, men have extolled heroes. People have identified with individuals who substituted for them and embodied the dreams they had of making a mark on the world. They lived through these heroes because they were unable to do what the heroes could do. The latter achieved great feats, sometimes selfishly, sometimes in such a manner as to reflect credit on humanity. A hero reputedly would have the strength of ten men, or he would possess enormous wisdom, or he would excel to an extraordinary degree in some other way. If accurate comparisons could have been made, his superiority probably would not have proved to be so great. But because most people were without education, power, and techniques of achievement, the advantages of heroes were magnified.

The most impressive characteristic of the hero was his audacity, his willingness to challenge. Like Job, he might question God; like Luther, he might challenge the church; like Columbus, he might challenge accepted knowledge; like American patriots, he might challenge the state. No one else dared do that. People revered him for his courage to tackle established institutions and to strike out into the unknown, and they were stirred as simple human beings by his accomplishments, for he did what they fancied themselves doing. Even the dullest men and women had dreams of doing what their heroes did.

This is why Adam stands at the base of all mythology. Instinctively, man knew that he was not born to be subjected to other men or forces autocratically. Intuition told him that he had a right to be his own man. Adam was the first great hero because he challenged God and authority; he ate the fruit of the forbidden tree, so that he himself became as God. Following Adam came such mythological heroes as Prometheus, Theseus, and Perseus—all challenging authority too. And there came the great Judeo-Christian leaders, such as Abraham, moving off on his own to start a new religion; Moses, taking people out of Egypt to found a new country; Jeremiah, threatening himself, his friends, God, and the state in order to stand on what seemed to him to be reason and justice. Isaiah, Amos, Micah, Ezra, Nehemiah, and others were cast in the same mold: strong, courageous individuals striking out against power and authority.

The legendary heroes of almost every country have been such men and women, from Joan of Arc, Cromwell, and Hampton to Simón Bolívar and Lenin. Almost every field of science has such heroes—Galileo, Copernicus, Servetus, to name but a few. Indeed, knowledge itself is often considered to be personified by Socrates claiming that man should question the power of the state and dying for the privilege. Probably the greatest challenger of all was Jesus, breaking up the whole structure of the Jewish church to make his own way. Paul and his Christian martyrs followed in his footsteps, and during the Reformation era, Calvin and Wesley followed in the martyrs' footsteps.

Always it was the hero who asserted his individuality, with the masses having that experience only vicariously, for the most part. They wanted to be like him, and they sensed that his example was mankind's destiny, but they dared not or could not assert themselves as he did.

This is the pattern that is being broken, with such enormous implications for America and the world. We are entering an age in which everyone can be—and has to be—his own hero, finding his own path, issuing his own challenge. We see this happening in many ways and places across the nation. There are student rebels on campuses, Ralph Naders in the marketplace, militant blacks in the ghettos, Gloria Steinems in women's rights movements, ecologists challenging industry in meetings with management. As for the arts, they seem to have settled into a state of seemingly permanent revolution: not only have many old rules been upset, but the concept of any rules at all is being challenged.

And this is going on around the world, stimulated by the example of the United States. In the Soviet Union, the intellectuals are challenging the Kremlin. In Italy, legislators are defying the Catholic Church. In Brazil, priests are challenging the military. In Japan, youth threatens age-old cultural traditions of conformity and obedience.

This new ethic of personal action, personal thinking, personal challenging, instead of heroism by proxy, will exert a profound effect upon our customs and institutions. The confrontations and acts of defiance we have seen during the last few years are only the beginning. Institutions as we have known them, operated along rigid authoritarian lines, simply cannot survive. Employees and shareowners will demand—and get—more influence in corporate management. Government powers will be shared more at the local, grass-roots levels. Students will participate more in the governance of educational institutions. Children will have more say in family matters; wives will divide authority more equally with their husbands.

But the impact on organization and structure is as nothing compared to the impact on personal lives. Here is where the real story lies. If there were only institutions at stake because of the new ethic, the prospects would be for evolutionary change. What makes the change epochal is that much more than organization is in the balance. The big question concerns the very soul of the ordinary American.

Crumbling Pillars

What is happening is not wholly a matter of individual choice, even though it represents the fruition of centuries of individual striving and sacrifice. Whether we like it or not, we are being forced into new roles by the disintegration of age-old patterns of decision-making.

Throughout the world and at every level of society we are witnessing the demise of omnipotent leaders. From the most ancient times up to the present, almost every group of people in existence at any time was subject to a strong, central leadership that decided how things would be. That leadership was considered to have special knowledge, special privileges, special powers, special abilities and capacities. Ruling by fear, force, magic, and mythology, it completely dominated the lives of constituents. It was rarely questioned or criticized— and when it was, the critic's life was in jeopardy. It dictated laws, beliefs, dress, morals, sexual relationships, work standards, social goals, military requirements, and many other things. Its assumption was that unless it whipped man into obedience, he would go back into the jungle from whence he had come; certainly he could not be expected to progress on his own.

Who were these rulers? One powerful group was ecclesiastical. Its immense powers are well documented in history books. Another group was political. The relatively few dictatorships left—in Communist China and Czechoslovakia, for instance— are vestiges of the dominant political pattern through most of human history.

Another powerful group was familial. Even in conservative families which retain some of the traditional authority structure, it is hard to remember that not long ago, in terms of recorded history, fathers had the right to decide life or death for family members. Their influence was so enormous that the state only occasionally could interfere in domestic relations. In that area, the family head was considered to be expressing the will of the church or society.

Another group of rulers consisted of tribal heads; except in a few parts of the earth, they are extinct now, but their authority was great for thousands of years. Then, too, there were military rulers; most of the time they were closely identified with, or perhaps the same as political rulers, at least at the top level, but subordinates in charge of operations—company commanders, captains of ships, and so forth—exercised almost unlimited power over the men in their command.

These various forms of authority ruling through fear and force have by no means disappeared. Here and there a church still exercises great power; there are still some dictatorships in the world; in some cultures the family head is still feared by family members; tribal rulership has carried over into the modern underworld, as readers and viewers of *The Godfather* know; and military rulers continue to have extreme powers in a number of areas. But where vestiges of the old forms remain, they are close to the "Going, going . . . gone" stage. Institutions with autocratic powers have lost their validity. People do not feel the need for them anymore or believe that they have all the answers.

And nowhere in the world is this more true than in the United States. Church leaders are no longer confident that they know the way to personal fulfillment and salvation. It is significant that whereas in 1957 only 14 percent of Americans believed that religion was "losing its influence on American life," according to the Gallup poll, by 1969 the figure had jumped to 70 percent ("one of the most dramatic reversals in opinion in the history of polling," according to George Gallup).[1] As for the state, its leaders are confused and torn by more problems than they can contend with, and they must bargain with an endless number of power groups, including scientists, civic action organizations, ethnic associations, and labor unions. Family power? It began to disintegrate when children became mobile. Heads of tribes have lost the mythologies they used to rely on for authority. Military rule has come under ever more suspicious scrutiny from the public.

In short, the old weapons of myth, miracle, fear, and awe have lost their power. People still succumb to fear and the lure of magic, but in fewer numbers, for shorter times, and with less conviction.

Thus we have arrived at a point where we know that there is no special truth, no special knowledge, no special rights for supernatural authorities. We are not willing to conform. We do not want authorities to tell us how to behave, dress, talk, think, or make love. We are increasingly unwilling even to let an employer tell us how to work or for what goals. As corporate executives know all too well, employees are pressing for the recognition of objectives other than corporate profit and productivity—for instance, such community goals as racial equality and ecology, and such desires of informal employee groups as the right to decide how their members will work together.

What trends and forces lie behind this disintegration of the traditional pillars of authority? Let me run over them quickly.

1. *The growth of reason and the scientific method.* Reason has been winning wider acceptance for two thousand years, and the scientific method, for some two hundred or three hundred years. Man wants to use his capacity to think, to explore, to understand. He doesn't want to rest in fear and wonderment over "miraculous" events; he wants to take them apart and know how they came to be. He will not be pushed; he insists on thinking for himself.

2. *Universal education.* The ordinary American has become capable of understanding as well as the public official, priest, mogul, or other ruler can. He must bow to no one in forming opinions and judgments. On the campus, students have been trained to think in relativistic terms. As pointed out by William G. Perry, Jr., in a major study at Harvard University,[2] whereas the professor used to ask questions that had right-

wrong answers—such as, "When was the battle of Hastings?"
or, "What did so-and-so say about a particular experiment?"—
now he asks, if the examination is about a poem, "What does
the poem mean to you, Mr. Sophomore?" or, "What do you
think Shakespeare, Freud, Dewey, Whitehead, and McLuhan
each would have said about the poem in the circumstances of
his life and times?"

3. *The democratization of wealth.* Money, and the power
that accompanies it, has become available to people from all
walks of life. The breakdown of feudalism and the rise of capitalism have given the average man financial means of using
the knowledge and know-how made available by education
and science.

4. *The breakup of local communities.* As the population has
multiplied, the mobility of the average person has increased
enormously. He is no longer tied to a community or a family
because of geography. What is more, he no longer *feels* tied to
the established institutions in the community where he re-
sides. For example, in religion the trend in Los Angeles is toward small enclaves of people meeting in homes and other
places instead of worshiping at churches and synagogues. The
same tendency can be seen in other major cities, and in such
fields as government and the arts as well as religion.

5. *Communication.* For the price of daily newspapers and a
television set, an American can keep up on developments and
cultures all over the world. No one needs to tell him what is
going on in other areas. He compares himself repeatedly with
people elsewhere; he is stimulated constantly to want the best
for himself.

6. *The development of law.* The function of law in Western
nations (and in more and more other countries) is to protect
the individual against encroachments by people in positions of
power and authority. Anglo-Saxon law first prescribed the

ways in which the king could function, then the actions of the church, the state, the family, and employers.

The combined result of these trends and forces has been to instill a new set of rights in the public consciousness. These rights were never legislated; they have never been written down in an official register. They have not been advanced under threats of violence, and it has not been felt necessary to resort to Voltaire's formula for progress, which was strangling the last king with the entrails of the last priest. But they are as real, and almost as well protected, as any rights in the Constitution. It is accepted that every American is entitled to: (*a*) know how he is made; (*b*) know where he comes from; (*c*) understand what contributes to his growth; (*d*) decide what his values are; (*e*) decide how he may best fulfill himself in society.

Without one official act we have in effect created a new "Bill of Rights" for all citizens.

Rise of the Self-Actualizers

This is why we no longer live vicariously through heroes. We believe in our own powers to decide and act. We will send no knights out to fight our battles for us. We must face the dragon ourselves, confront Medusa ourselves, explore the depths of the soul ourselves, imagine the future both during and after life as best we can.

We will be self-actualizers, to use Abraham Maslow's term. In *Toward a Psychology of Being* he put it this way:

Self-actualizing people are relatively unfrightened by the unknown, the mysterious, the puzzling, and often are positively attracted by it. . . . They do not neglect the unknown, or deny it, or run away from it, or try to make believe it is really known, nor do they organize, dichotomize, or rubricize it prematurely. They do not cling to the familiar, nor is their quest for the truth a catastrophic need for certainty, safety, definiteness, and order. . . . They can be, when the total objective situation calls for it, comfortably disorderly, sloppy, anarchic, chaotic, vague, doubtful, uncertain, indefinite, approximate, inexact, or inaccurate.[3]

The young people have a phrase for this new attitude—"Do your own thing." They mean that every person has something unique to do, and he cannot let a proxy do it for him. He must feel, sense, touch, understand, take to himself, and express himself in his own way. Write your own book, they tell us. Write your own poem, paint your own picture, think your own thoughts, build your own church. Not one hundred or two hundred gifted leaders but *millions* of people have the right and the freedom to become heroes.

I have no way of predicting what the outcome of this development will be, but I know what the *possibilities* are. They range from catastrophe to the realization of the oldest and fondest dreams of Americans. I think Joseph Campbell has expressed the alternatives well:

> Out beyond those walls in the uncharted forest night where the terrible wind of God blows directly on the questing undefended soul, tangled ways may lead to madness. They may also lead, however, to all those things that go to make heaven and earth.[4]

2

The New Dilemma

Now that man is finally on his own, he is discovering a truth that never occurred to him during the thousands of years when he lived vicariously through his heroes. Freedom to "do your own thing," he is learning to his surprise, does not meet the need for a richer life either.

In 1965 Floyd Patterson was interviewed by a reporter for a national magazine. Patterson, you will remember, was the youngest man ever to win the world's heavyweight boxing championship. At the time of the interview, he was also the only boxer ever to have lost the title and won it back again (in 1961). He was a millionaire. He had health, family, worldwide respect, and interesting prospects for future work.

But he was not heavyweight champion of the world. He had lost the title again (to Sonny Liston in 1962).

"Now, if I were a wise man," he told the reporter, "I would retire. But I'm not a wise man. I'm just like everyone else. I want one more chance. Just one more chance." Near the end of the interview he said: "All my life I've been waiting, waiting, waiting. Waiting for the next fight. Waiting for the decision. Waiting for the next fight again. And now my children are growing up and life is passing me by and I'm still waiting, but now I've got something to wait for."

Does Anyone Ever Have Enough?

Floyd Patterson meant to speak only for himself. In truth, he spoke for millions of self-actualizers before and since then. It is not enough for the world to tell you that you can be your own hero. It is not enough to have the education, financial means, and know-how needed to go out and seek a challenging goal. It is not enough even to achieve the goal. People all over are discovering this irony now, and they cannot believe it. So, like Patterson, they decide that they need to make another run. Then they will be able to relax with honor and dignity—or so they say.

I know people who have enormous incomes (I do not use the word "enormous" lightly), and have had them for years, but they find that the incomes are not enough. They have trust funds in case anything goes wrong with their jobs or businesses; they have plenty of insurance; they have large savings. But those backups are not enough either.

On Thanksgiving night in 1971 a major television network offered a documentary about a fine family I know who live in Birmingham, Michigan, an affluent suburb of Detroit. Viewers of this program saw a fortunate group. It possessed no apparent problems and lived in considerable comfort. The children were bright and personable. Yet, as reviewers noted, the family seemed vaguely unhappy and there appeared to be a meaningless quality about the life they led. In the end, the family moved to a bigger, more expensive house in an even more affluent suburb, as if this move might somehow counteract the malaise they felt.

When you were young you may have thought to yourself, "If only I had $50,000 in securities, I'd have enough." Later, if you were fortunate, you might have accumulated that amount.

"Well, $50,000 doesn't look like so much," you said then. "I really ought to have $100,000. With $100,000 out at interest of 5 percent, I could live on that." But when you get $100,000 saved up you don't talk anymore in terms of $5,000 a year to live on. By that time you need a quarter of a million dollars in capital to keep up with the people you know. On and on this process goes—all of us are familiar with it. I know people who are poor on three or four million dollars of capital. They worry about being hard up, they complain about it, they go without little pleasures to prove it.

It isn't only money that leaves us feeling this way. The same goes for countless other things. Take friendship, for instance. If you have a friend now, you have the whole infinite realm of friendship to enjoy. But have you ever known a person who sought more friendship who ever got enough of it? One friend does not suffice—you need another. And then another. There are men and women who have hundreds of friends, and still they want more. They aren't satisfied with one. They wouldn't be satisfied with a thousand. And so, no matter how large their communities have grown, or how select their country clubs have become, they do not have enough.

Some people have this problem with respect to sex. Sex is a very physical thing, yet it is an intangible in the sense that those who keep seeking more of it are most likely looking not for physical release but for the power, sense of manhood, or sense of conquest that sex brings. But if a normal amount of sex isn't enough for them, more will not be the answer. If I could have just this person . . . , they keep thinking. Have you ever known a great lover who ever got enough sex?

In our Western culture today young people put a great deal of emphasis on music, noise, activity. They want to be doing, doing, doing! They substitute activity for significance. I am reminded of a television program, shown several years ago,

called *The Way Out Man.* This was a story about some researchers who gave a community of mice in a laboratory all
the food and drink they could take. Ideal surroundings and
facilities were provided. The mice started out having a marvelous time. They ate, they drank, they grew big and strong,
they had community nurseries so that their beautiful mice
children would get the best of everything too. They had sexual relations wherever and whenever they wanted them.

But then they began to stop breeding. Homosexualism increased. The confusion, the noise, the contacts began to put
them into states of catatonic shock, wherein they experienced
but did not see, feel, or hear. Then the mice began crawling
up the walls and hanging themselves to death on pegs in order
to get away from all the activity and clamor.

Is this a preview of what is happening to our civilization?
If you look around you today, you can see possible signs of it:
people who are educated and able to participate but are shutting themselves off from real involvement in their communities, going into states of semishock so that they will not be disturbed, finding intellectual and emotional retreats for
themselves so that they can avoid further experiencing and
feeling. It is hoped that our civilization will not go to that extreme—I do not believe that it will. But I know that noise and
activity are things that do not satisfy enough either, if they do
not satisfy now.

Like sex and money, organization is one of the most physical of things, but also an intangible in the respect that it becomes a substitute for other needs, such as dominance and
control. If you are one of those who seeks ever more efficient
organization at a company or a hospital, ever larger spheres of
authority and command, you never get enough. Each new addition or step brings a momentary glow of satisfaction, but
then you begin to cast your eyes on the next possibility. "If

only I could have that," you say to yourself, "*then* I would be satisfied." You can search all the libraries of business, political, and military history and find no good example, I suspect, of an organizer who, dissatisfied early in his career with the efficiency or size of his organization, ever became satisfied later.

In short, man finds himself confronting a true dilemma: In the past it was not enough *not* to be a hero, but neither is it enough today to be one. The old American dream of individualism has been realized as it was never realized before—and it solves nothing. We are free to run to a goal and we do run, but somehow or other we never seem to get somewhere that satisfies us. This is not just a simple, passing foolishness of man; it is a tragedy. For we go down to our graves dissatisfied, "still waiting," as Floyd Patterson put it. Americans are the winningest nation on earth, but that has not made us happier.

The Shadow of Futility

In fact, it may be that the new individualism has served to make us *less* happy. No matter how plentifully we achieve, we feel as inadequate as ever. In view of our whetted aspirations, that leaves us with a larger margin of disappointment.

We take it out on ourselves. Few traits of modern Americans have impressed me as frequently and poignantly as their low opinions of their worth. For example, as cities go, Grand Rapids has more than its share of healthy, active, successful, well-to-do people. But when, in the privacy of an office, they bare their feelings about themselves to me, they reveal chagrin, disappointment, and even self-contempt. Strangest of all, they feel that, despite all their activities, they are not leading useful lives. Considerable experience with this reaction has convinced me of the truth of an observation made by Jacob Bronowski in his discerning book *The Face of Violence*. "The shadow of futility," Bronowski says, "follows every man in the modern world." [5]

The implications of this are more serious than we may be inclined to think. "A feeling of uselessness," said the great nineteenth-century philosopher Thomas Huxley, "is the severest shock that the human system can endure." In Americans, the feeling is most readily seen among middle-aged people. Whether we serve as attorneys, doctors, ministers, social workers, school committee officials, or mothers, the time comes when we can no longer "produce" and, by such action, draw recognition. We were "somebody"; now we are "nobody." I am thinking of the man who was the pillar of the church or of the community. I am thinking of the woman who was once beautiful—and therefore extremely desirable, according to our society. I am thinking of the mother whose children are no longer with her. People like these become overwhelmed with a sense of emptiness and futility of existence. "What's the use? I'm no longer needed, I no longer have a function to fulfill." I have heard this reaction over and over again for years, from mature and intelligent people. Indeed, I know of no one who has escaped this feeling in middle age. "Who am I? What have I done? What happened to my dreams—*and who really cares?*" Their eyes lose their sparkle, their bodies lose their tension, they begin to die.

But middle-aged people are not alone. All too well I know that adolescents have their own versions of the same problem. Although commanding fresh and marvelous powers and with wonderful careers ahead of them, they feel that they don't belong, that there is nothing really important for them to do. "If I were no longer here," they ask me, "what difference would it make?"

This malaise shows up in diverse ways. It shows up in our mental institutions. Studies indicate that three out of every five people experience emotional breakdown one or more times during their lives—and that figure is increasing! The phenomenon shows up in statistics of hospital-bed occupation. It is difficult to exaggerate the amount of diagnosable physical illness that is due originally to the feeling of uselessness. I know that the figure might run as high as 90 percent in the general hospitals of a city such as Grand Rapids! The "Who really cares?" feeling also shows up in alcoholism. Is there anyone who does not know an alcoholic in his circle of family, close friends, and immediate neighbors? The alcoholic tries to forget that he is a nobody by crawling into a state of forgetfulness.

What about the alarming increase in the use of drugs? That is another manifestation of uselessness feelings. No one who finds joy and vitality in daily existence resorts to drugs. Or consider the suicide rate. Ironically, so many persons who commit suicide are the very ones who apparently have the most to be thankful for—Ernest Hemingway, who got up one morning in one of the most beautiful places in the world and took a gun from the rack and blew his head off; Marilyn Monroe, who escaped from the despair of stardom by taking an overdose of drugs; and James Forrestal, who at the height of his power over the military-industrial complex hurtled to his death from a high building, to name but a few.

What about the crowds who surround the demagogues in various parts of the world? Like the crowds that surrounded Hitler and Mussolini, they are there trying to escape the feelings of being nobodies. As Albert Speer, Hitler's minister of armaments, has made clear, it was not just the Nazi leader's personality but the followers' needs to feel important that drew them to him. And is there any real difference between that sort of crowd and the crowds of motorcyclists such as the "Outlaws" that terrorize neighborhoods? I remember a report in the *Detroit Free Press*, several years ago, describing how the police found swastikas and Nazi flags after moving out a group of fifteen hundred "Outlaws" in Detroit. When asked why they used those symbols, members of the gang answered: "Well, the Nazis were losers and we're losers too, so why not? We use it to bug people, to blow them out, so they'll notice us." Similar psychologies characterize the city-street gangs that maim and kill innocent people and some of the campus mobs that overturn cars, throw bricks through windows, and blow up buildings. In their own ways they are doing the same thing the alcoholics, drug addicts, and psychosomatic patients are doing—trying to escape the shadow of futility that hovers over them.

Now, in diagnosing these breakdowns as failures of our culture, and in particular as failures of self-actualization as we understand it, I do not mean to minimize other aggravating factors. I am perfectly aware of what it means to be one student of forty thousand on the University of Michigan campus. I know of the massive congestion in cities and suburbs. I recognize the impact of increasing complexity in the modern world, which makes it almost impossible for anyone to master all the angles of the war in Vietnam or of combating inflation or pollution. I appreciate the human implications of a technology that substitutes teaching machines for teachers and automation for individual craftsmanship. I recognize the deterioration in communities and neighborly relationships. I know what it means to be more important to others as a Social Security number than as a human being with a Christian name. I know about the traumatic effect on whites and blacks alike of racial problems.

Trends such as these have deepened the shadow of futility

described by Bronowski and accentuated the feelings of use-lessness that overwhelm us. But the malaise described is not confined to America; it is found in other nations blessedly free of swiftly expanding populations, racial explosions, and Vietnams. It is found in France, which recently reported its first cases ever of teen-age self-immolation (in Lille); it is found in Holland, Germany, "utopian" Sweden, and Japan. Significantly, the poetry of such countries reflects bitterness and discouragement too.[6] In short, among industrially advanced nations, the tendency seems to be universal.

Moreover, the fact stands that, had you sat down a hundred or five hundred years ago with an average person in a Western nation, and described to him the opportunities for personal achievement that are available to the average man or woman today, he would surely have thought, That is all I could ever wish for!

Our society is incredibly rich with opportunities for full, happy, exciting lives. Like Floyd Patterson, we keep running after them, exploiting them, losing them, waiting for another chance. But no matter how hard and fast we run, no matter how long we wait, the satisfaction never seems to materialize. The horizon is always out there receding—and we are perfectly right in thinking that we are never going to get to it. Never. I have a poem by Stephen Crane which expresses the thought in another way:

> I saw a man pursuing the horizon;
> Round and round they sped.
> I was disturbed at this;
> I accosted the man.
> "It is futile," I said,
> "You can never—"
> "You lie," he cried.
> And ran on.

No More Miracles

The mood of frustration and depression that has settled over us in the midst of unprecedented affluence and opportunity shows up in many ways, and one of them in particular seems quite significant to me. It is not only a symptom or manifestation of the problem, I feel, but also a cause: once created (as it has been steadily in recent times), it tends to regenerate the causes that produced it in the first place.

As a people we have lost the sense of mystery, wonder, reverence, and awe that our ancestors used to have. There seems to be less and less that we can refer to as the great unknown, less and less that is not laid bare in the ruthless light of science. And so, more frequently than at any previous point in history, I am sure, we hear people make statements such as:

"What's so wonderful about the emergence of a butterfly from a cocoon? After all, it's perfectly natural. All butterflies emerge from cocoons."

"Why all the fuss over babies? They're a perfectly natural and common event. Babies have been acting like that for years!"

"If you have seen one sequoia, you've seen them all. There's no mystery about them."

As another illustration, suppose you are trying to remember something, but the fact will not come to you. You think of associations that might help, you pick connections here and there that might jog your memory, and gradually the idea comes nearer the surface. Then all of a sudden you exclaim, "I have it!" But there is nothing astonishing about such a process today. "Why, that's just memory," people say. "Don't you understand memory? There's a place on the brain, you know—it can be isolated. Memory is a neural response and it's simple enough. Your knowledge is stored there chemically."

In short, there do not seem to be miracles or surprises anymore. We understand how everything is made, how it operates, and what its capacities are—all the question marks have been stripped away, reducing the life or thing to the commonplace. "What else is new?" has become a favorite expression. And how many statements we make begin with such words as, "It's only a . . ." or, "That's just another . . ."?

Of course, the reason for all this is not hard to find. We are in the midst of a scientific age. The ideals of science are rigor of method, insistence on procedure, total and complete objectivity. There is no room in scientific adventure for the sentimental or the romantic. Nothing must remain hidden. To the greatest extent possible, all aspects of life are laid out on the laboratory table for examination, classification, measuring, testing, and retesting, until the last false assumption or unproved speculation is tossed away. And as every schoolchild and college student knows, scientific method is no longer exclusive to the physical and life sciences. It is part of the approach to the social sciences as well, and now even to sports.

With the loss of the miraculous has gone loss of celebration, ritual, decoration, and color in our lives. Rites and festivity have come to appear a little absurd to many of us. (I do not refer to occultism, which has sprung up here, there, and everywhere and has become a new religion. Occultism is a form of fantasy, and there is no shortage of fantasy in the modern world, as any moviegoer knows.) I notice more and more people looking with peculiar smiles upon personal, family, or community celebrations, as though they were a little childish. Romance is regarded as out-of-date, along with extravaganzas of the spirit.

Parades? They used to be festive events of importance to communities. Now they are more often planned as political, social, or economic weapons. No longer are they a source of delight to children—high points of the year. What has happened to Easter? It is a big-collection day in many of the churches, but the color and the exuberance are gone. Even the celebration of Christmas has come under suspicion. People find less and less time for it; the festivity has been abbreviated (though the holidays may be longer). We take less time to decorate our gifts, we have toned down the once-colorful ceremonials, we regard as absurd the notion that there is a mystery about Christmas. Scientists have explained that the star of Bethlehem was an ordinary star!

The Sacred and the Secular

Now, the point of all this is not to renew interest in the supernatural. Let us remember that the men and women of ancient times did not look beyond this world for objects and symbols to revere. They found sacred things in their everyday lives—the most ordinary things they could invest with sanctity. There were millions of bushes just like the one Moses saw burning in the wilderness. Some of the stones they honored were just stones. They treasured certain animals of species that had always lived in the area and always would.

It was the common, everyday world that filled them with

wonder. Incapable of approaching the world with modern scientific efficiency, they found beauty and wonder in simple things on which they depended for their existence. When they thought and found something significant in their minds, it could be a revelation, an illumination, a gift from God. When they experienced wonder and awe, their lives became richer.

Today we refer to such experiences as childish. But we do so with derision—and there, I believe, is where we make a mistake. Childish it may have been, for a child does indeed romanticize objects and beings about him. He knows that the dog does not really talk, but because he imagines that it speaks to him, the child invests it with the power of speech. The child knows that the pillow is not really a lion that roars in the jungle, but he makes that pillow a lion. His imagination can do this to almost anything—a blanket, a battered toy, a doll, or maybe just a stone. There can be treasure and mystery anywhere in the child's world. We adults cannot see them, but that does not make them invalid.

The fact is that as we grow older we lose interest in seeing things as a child might, not so much because we are smarter and more knowledgeable but because of our changing system of values. As adults, we feel we must be practical and accurate. We must be able to prove what we see. We have to hurry, and the faster we move, the less any one part of the world means to us. We no longer have the time or the inclination to stop, look, and wonder.

Yet the miracles are still there. It is not science that has eliminated them, but our hearts and minds. The butterfly emerging from the cocoon is still a miracle; we know far more than the ancients did about how it happens, but the fact that it *does* happen is a mystery. The production of an infant by two human beings is still miraculous—no less believable because of the volumes of scientific knowledge on obstetrics. The fact that doctors can find no two human beings who have exactly the same nervous system—even after billions of people have lived—is a very remarkable fact to contemplate. There are astonishing facts about bacteria, and the more they are studied, the more astonishing they seem. The nature of time is an enigma. One could go on and on with such examples, but surely my point must be clear: the mysteries are as abundant as ever, only we do not have the time or the inclination to wonder about them anymore.

I have no quarrel with the scientific mind. In fact, I believe that it should be used more widely than it is, not less so. But I have seen too much of what it does to people when it absorbs, encompasses, and rules their point of view. *The loss of the miraculous from our world is a deadly thing for the human spirit.* An appalling proportion of Americans seem to be bored to death. They are buyers or prospective buyers of tranquilizers to shut out the frustration of doing nothing and of being surprised by nothing—nobody ever discovers anything out of boredom. They make up part of the market for pep pills to provide a little energy, false interest, and excitement to take the grayness of the day away. If they dance, they are the ones who play it cool, showing no expression, awed by nothing and no one. They are candidates, I am afraid, for any charlatan or self-proclaimed messiah who can break through their apathy.

The tragedy of the unsurprisable, unastonishable, completely practical man is well known to our poets. Simon and Garfunkel sing of a very fine citizen who had made good in the community, was highly respected, and did the right things, such as giving freely to charity. So people's minds were filled with wonder, Simon and Garfunkel sing, when the evening headlines read that the man "went home last night and put a bullet through his head." [7] Life held everything for him but enchantment.

The poet John Ciardi once made these observations:

> There is no poetry for the practical man [the "doer," the paragon of business efficiency]. . . . Let him spend too much of his life at the mechanics of practicality and either he must become something less than a man, or his very mechanical efficiency will become impaired by the frustrations stored up in his irrational personality. An ulcer, gentlemen, is an unkissed imagination taking its revenge for having been jilted. It is an unwritten poem, a neglected music, an unpainted water color, an undanced dance. It is a declaration from the mankind of man that a clear spring of joy has not been tapped, and that it must break through, muddily, on its own.[8]

How Much Can You Manage?

One of the most tragic aspects of our malaise is our preoccupation with management and control. It seems to have become a part of our culture. It is as if we try to compensate for the loss of wonder by being efficient and dominating. Such a reaction is a disease that can destroy us personally and could even destroy us as a people. For instance, consider how often we hear exchanges such as the following:

"How are things, Joe?"

"Fine, fine."

"Everything under control?"

"Yep, everything's under control. I'm sitting on top of the world."

We believe that we have to have things under control before we can do a good job. We judge a person by how much he has under control and how closely he watches it. We want people who will take a job, organize it, and efficiently manage it. We say to our friends in critical appraisal: "What's the matter? Can't you manage it?" We almost never stop to question whether or not they *should* manage it. Men say, not just in humor or joshingly: "What's the matter? Can't you manage your wife?" Something is wrong with a man who cannot manage his wife so that he can get to do what he wants to do! And I am sure that it is the same in feminine circles; the assumption is that they ought to be able to manage their husbands, each in her own way, of course, but each sure that she has him under control.

We manage our work; we manage, control, and arrange our friendships and families; we manage and control our thinking and feelings. Are not these activities the expressions of civilization? Only barbarians do not control!

Of course, this approach brings many rewards. It enables us to be efficient. Also, if we know what is going to happen and are prepared for it, we are not thrown off step. We know we have to produce the parts, and we have available all kinds of resources for contingencies so that nothing unexpected will interfere with efficient production. This is efficiency in a factory, in city management, in our homes, and with our friends and children.

Moreover, management and organization give us a feeling of purpose and mission which we find terribly necessary. And if we begin to feel purposeless and lost (which we occasionally do), then we start organizing again to become more efficient so that we know better what we are doing. With moving toward the goal comes a sense of power.

All this is supposed to bring us peace of mind. Ask Americans what they mean by "peace of mind" and they will describe it as an assurance that what they are doing is all right. It is faith and confidence that they are moving in the right direction and everything around is in its place.

However, in reality there is almost no virtue in the arrogance that assumes a person has "got it made," is "sitting on top of the world," and has "everything under control." When we act this way we assume the role of God, and in a human being that is destructive. One does not have to be a national leader manipulating great continents of people in order to exhibit this kind of arrogance. A little man can be just as arrogant as a Hitler or a Stalin even though his scene of operation is smaller.

Management and control are not good because they encourage us to cut down and cut off. If we feel we have to manage or break down, we cut back on the scope of our activities. If we cannot handle our relationships, we cut down on the number and size of them. If there is some friend we cannot handle, we get rid of him. If there is some information and knowledge that is too confusing, we forget about it.

Does all this *really* lead to peace of mind? If it is true that we are finite creatures in an infinite universe, then we only deceive ourselves when we think in terms of control. No matter how well we seem to have got our lives managed, *we know we haven't really and are afraid.* I have watched this time and again. We get something all nicely arranged but worry because we know it can be jumbled again. So we walk around with anxiety in our hearts wondering when the blow is going to come.

In short, we manage ourselves into spiritual poverty because the things that we can control are things that are within our range now. But unless we run into things we cannot control, how can we enlarge our range? There is an infinite world around, but how are we going to find it if we are always manipulating people, closing the doors, pulling down the curtains so that we can keep our world manageable? If we cannot grow except by enlarging our pattern, that means our pattern has to be broken. We must violate our order, efficiency, and management; we must expose ourselves to the abyss, the destructive, and the unknown.

Paradoxically, real peace of mind comes not to the person who has the world by the tail but to the person who is wrestling, confused, searching, and eager, who wants to manage and will not do so. This person lives in a world of mystery, wonder, miracles—and shattering awakenings. He does not live with life all wrapped up like a Christmas box.

Management and control are wonderful values if we keep them in narrow bounds. But let them become part of our feelings about life and our philosophy about how to relate to the world around us, and they will surely diminish the wonders that make life worth living. That is what has been happening in our society.

Part II

THE POWER
OF THE SPIRIT

4

A Modern Version of the Spirit

On the face of it, the situation described may look discouraging, possibly hopeless. Certainly there is widespread pessimism about the future among many sensitive, perceptive men and women today.

I believe that there is an answer to the American predicament. This answer cannot be achieved by institutions, although they can help; nor by national and local leaders, though they can help too. It can be found only by individuals —remember, the predicament is an intensely individual one. The answer is a spiritual approach to life. It is to develop spirituality in a specific sense of the word—a sense that can be communicated, analyzed, discussed, and debated as clearly as can any other well-defined concept. Spirituality, as I shall discuss it in this book, is not vague, fuzzy, or beyond reason. Nor is it an old-fashioned, fundamentalist, or sentimental approach. The ideas to be described would not readily have been recognized in times past, although some great insights concerning them come from peoples of the past.

Every age must paint its own pictures. In doing so, it does not repudiate the pictures of earlier ages; it may revere them and learn from them. But as times change and methods of perception change, feelings and knowledge and emphasis change, and so people express themselves differently. This is the way it is with painting, music, writing, teaching, organization, leadership, and other arts. This is also the way it should be with understanding the spirit.

For modern Americans, a supernatural concept of the spirit does not answer the problem of emptiness and dissatisfaction with life's activities. It may be valid for other purposes, but not for this one. Nor will a mystical version of the spirit suffice. There is, I know, a trend to more mysticism and occultism in religion, but it will not satisfy many people for very long in this day and age. Nor can an emotional or inspirational interpretation of spirituality answer modern man's problem. Unfortunately, much of the literature on the spirit deals with it as a feeling of contentment, a tingling sensation, or a buildup of enthusiasm. Spirituality does indeed involve our feelings, and it may evoke great wonder when we hear beautiful music, see a fine work of art, or watch a splendid sunset— but it is not the feeling itself. The spiritual approach, as modern Americans need to think of it, is not at all sentimental, mystical, or supernatural. In fact, its qualities are the opposite of those characteristics.

Relatedness and Meaning

What is the spirit? My answer may surprise many people and disappoint others (at least, at first). We are in the habit of looking for things, shapes, and activities—and the spirit is none of these. To use an analogy from scientific thought, we cannot define spirituality in Newtonian terms; we must use terms more akin to Einsteinian thought, or to the concepts of quantum physics. We do not have to go hunting for the elements of the spirit or create them. They are all around us all of the time, as common as energy and the air we breathe.

Spirituality is the combination of thinking and feeling that enables a person to understand people and things in relationship. It takes place only through thinking *and* feeling; just as there can be no nuclear fusion without combining the hydrogen isotopes, deuterium and tritium, so there can be no spiritual fusion without bringing together the conscious and unconscious, the intellect and the visceral senses, mind and body. Also, as the definition indicates, spirituality deals only with relatedness. The greater and deeper one's awareness of the relatedness of life, the greater and deeper is one's spirit.

Spirituality in this sense goes *directly* to the heart of the American predicament as earlier described. One way to demonstrate this is to refer to a well-known finding in the field of psychiatry. Carl Jung, Rollo May, and other leading psychiatrists have repeatedly found that among patients troubled by a sense of emptiness and futility, the central problem is lack of awareness of how activities, people, and things relate to one another. Indeed, Carl Jung used to say that he had no patients over the age of thirty-five whose problem was not basically an incapacity to see relationships. Of course, they were aware of the relatedness about them to some extent, or they would have been totally mad, but their awareness was at a low level.

Now, what makes this significant is the nature of the human mind. Thought is itself an awareness of interrelationships. As Jung and others have noted, it is impossible for a person to be conscious of disconnected events. Consciousness *means* that events are seen as possessing some degree of relationship. It is always tying one thing to another, this day to yesterday or tomorrow, one person to another, and so on.

To use an illustration: For some months a child shows no sense of consciousness. Then suddenly, it begins to relate events to itself as a person; it becomes "I." Beginning with this miracle, the child grows in ability to relate people and things to each other, moving from the darkness of unconsciousness into ever greater awareness as an adult. The process takes place naturally at first, without conscious effort. Later, specific effort and education may be needed. If the process is interrupted or distorted for some reason, the person comes in need of psychiatric care. Information, knowledge, technical skills, awards, and achievements as such do not help. The person's capacity to *relate* things is what has to be renewed. Internal barriers in his perception of reality must be removed.

Similarly, the emptiness of our lives is the result of seeing people and things in relative isolation. Nothing seems to lead much of anywhere. This is another way of saying that spirituality is lacking. Where the spirit is full, *any* life, however drab or limited or restricted in a material sense, is rich and rewarding because it is seen in relationship, and therefore meaningfully. As the Beatles say in one of their songs, you do not need to travel to know the wonders of the earth.[9]

Does this explanation make the spirit seem impersonal and "scientific"? That may be the result of my effort to show the reality of the spirit, to bring it into the domain of rational discussion and learning. But let me assure the reader that spirituality is anything but cold and impersonal in actual life. The spirit just described is what enables a person to experience joy as it can never be experienced otherwise—beyond sensuous delight, beyond ecstasy, beyond the pleasures of triumph and applause. The spirit just described was what warmed the hearts of the saints and led to what was perhaps the most incredible act of understanding of all time—Jesus on the cross saying "Father, forgive them; for they know not what they do."

Because of its emphasis on organic wholeness, spirituality represents a radical break with the tradition of industrial civilization, where, as with the production line, each person does a limited piece of work and passes it on to others, until in the end all the parts are put together in a completed product. It is a break with the tradition of specialization, of the mechanical philosophy of life whereby we think, I do this and you do that, and together we'll make this society.

What is there about thinking and feeling in combination that makes spirituality possible? (Some people prefer to use "knowing" or "awareness" as a substitute for "thinking" in the definition given. Others prefer the expression "mind and body" to "thinking and feeling." I consider them equally satisfactory and will use them interchangeably in describing aspects of the spirit.) Thinking is indispensable to the combination because this is mainly what separates man from the animal. Feeling is indispensable because this is what separates man from the machine; in its absence, a computer might conceivably be programmed to do the job as well as a human could. Also, as we shall see in the next chapter, feeling has such deep roots in human personality that, without it, rational thought would be insignificant.

The role of fusion is to make thought and feeling indistinguishable from each other. Spirituality is not five parts thought and five parts feeling, but ten parts of thought-feeling recognizable only as a new form. This is what makes it possible for a person to be "whole" in his understanding at a particular moment—a sensation of well-being and harmony with the universe which, while fleeting, is long remembered afterward. The person is not fragmented, dichotomized, or alienated; physiologically, it might be said that there is no conflict between his "gut feel" and his rational choice. Such wholeness is rare for people but easy for animals, which do not have minds to distract or confuse them.

Let us take an illustration. I offer illustrations here and later in this book with some fear and misgiving because any of them could quite conceivably be symptomatic of different conditions from the point I am trying to illustrate. When, for example, you feel love for your fellowman you may think you are experiencing a deep and abiding affection for people, when in reality you are experiencing the results of one drink too many. Or your aversion to a certain tendency of youth may not be a lack of understanding, as it seems to others, but the effect of a nervous stomach or an unpleasant association in your childhood. Anyone employing illustrations runs the risk that a given example could be explained in such a way. I hope that it will be understood, therefore, that the examples used here are not intended to prove the arguments but to help convey meaning.

For a very simple example, suppose you are on a hunting trip. You have a marvelous time with your comrades, and you come back saying that there is nothing in the world like hunting. It is the finest experience a person can have! Now, you are not describing the experience of hunting. You are really talking about the comradeship, joy, and delight of doing something together with friends, with people who are free and easy and who understand one another and work together in an attitude of mutual aid and cooperation. There is harmony and a feeling of oneness in the group. Some people call it love.

In this sense the hunting trip is a spiritual experience. In it, thinking is important because the members have to know something about hunting, each other, and their interrelationships. You don't just put any group of people together, place them out in the woods with guns, and produce a pleasurable hunting expedition! And even when you get the right group, the members have to keep working together with their minds, because if they become forgetful of one another, or motivated by desires to dominate or exploit, the cohesiveness of the group will not last very long.

Feeling is also very important in the experience. When you came back talking about what a marvelous time you had, you referred to pleasures that you had experienced viscerally—"in your heart," some would say, or "in your whole being." No matter how satisfying that trip was in an intellectual way because things went without a hitch, on time (if they did go on time), and with deer being brought back, it would have been only a sterile exercise but for the feelings of satisfaction it produced.

The most important thing of all, however, was the thought-feeling fusion. You didn't think to yourself, I will relate to the group in such-and-such a way because experiments in group dynamics prove that is the most productive way. (People do that sometimes and we're all too aware of their method!) And you didn't just go along with the group and entertain sensations—sight, sound, smell, hot-cold feelings, and touch. To be sure, you were acutely aware *at times* of sensations—for instance, the first awareness of woods all around you, or the taste of the first cup of coffee in the morning. And you were fully aware at other times that you were working out a problem with your mind—when you were arguing about a cooking duty rotation, for instance, or deciding that you had better not tell one person about what another had done earlier in the day. But what made the trip memorable for you was a mind-body combination of pleasure and meaning that was more than the sum of both.

This combination of experience was more significant to you than were any of the purely physical sensations *or* mental exercises individually. In the future it will have more influence on you than the individual elements will, you will remember it longer, and, if you have enough such experiences, it will profoundly influence your personality and relations with other people. That is why we give it a different name: *spirit*.

Of course, the hunting trip is but an example. You could have had much the same experience on a fishing trip, with an athletic team, in your family, in business, or in military service.

Implications for Creativity

The more sensitively a spiritual person sees and feels, the greater the possibility of exercising qualities necessary for survival or enrichment. For instance, if I do not see the hurt look or beaten posture of another person, or hear the cry for help in his voice, or catch his mood of responsiveness or desire, I will not be able to work so productively with him. The more the nuances are caught and reflected back in our relationship, the more the possibilities of creative interplay. Again, spiritual awareness is vital to the building of civilization. The automobile requires roads; roads create easy access, which in turn makes possible centralized cities, suburban flight, and a whole new environment. Everything and everyone is affected. If we are not aware of these dynamic relationships in our planning, we create the stupid, impossible cities that burden us today, with all of their crime, corruption, and other problems. For still another illustration, consider the ecology movement. The quality of our actions affecting animal and bird life is dependent upon the depth of our spiritual awareness. Are we members of Trout Unlimited so we will have more fishing or because we recognize that man cannot be divorced from nature? It makes a great deal of difference in our behavior.

All this is another way of emphasizing that spirituality is not a separate realm of religion or life that has its own rules and standards competing with other standards. Rather, it is a quality of life that impregnates every action and thought of a person, is present on every occasion, and is subject to the same factors that influence his behavior in other respects (e.g., buoyant health or hunger). It offers us no escape from the everyday demands of civilized existence. Technical problems must still be solved with the best of technical know-how. Human relationships still require time and patience, and even then continue to go awry. In one sense, therefore, we see the same things we would see without spirituality. But we see them differently, and so we are different. And in that difference lies the key to heaven or hell on earth.

Perhaps the supreme illustration in our culture of seeing, feeling, and understanding the whole organic relatedness of mankind was the life of Jesus. As for the arch-symbol for all time of the opposite of spirit, that may be Stalin. Working sincerely for an ideal of efficiency, discipline, and organization, but with scarcely more feeling than a monster computer, Stalin could kill kulaks by the million. Utilizing intellect only, he could see only the parts—and everything, including people, *were* parts. It made perfectly good sense to him to discard a part, whether it was a group of military or economic enemies or a drain on the state treasury, when it interfered with the national machine.

Jesus and Stalin personify the range of spirituality, from very high to very low. The rest of us are somewhere in between. If we were to spend the rest of our lifetimes working at it, we could not come very close to either extreme. But if we move a little in one direction or the other—and there is no doubt but that we can if we want to—the result will be profound in terms of individual satisfaction. And if many of us were to move a little in one direction or the other, the result would be as momentous from society's standpoint as the coming of another saint or another Stalin.

The Validity
of the Irrational

The spirit is made up of ordinary elements, as we have just seen, yet it has an extraordinary effect on the individual. It is a source of creative, transformational powers far greater than those which can be developed by any training program, creativity technique, or personality-building method we know of. The man-made approaches may turn an average salesman into an extraordinary one, or a mediocre inventor into a more successful one, but that is all they want to claim. They cannot make life worthwhile, which is what the spirit can do for an individual, or provide a framework for decisions that will save a people from self-destruction, which is what a spiritual approach can do for society.

And the spirit is far more powerful than reason. Whether reason is defined in terms of scientific method, logical processes, empirical analysis, or some other such approach or combination of approaches, it cannot equal the spirit as a source of creative understanding and development. The difference between a person great in spirit and a person great only in reason is the difference between, say, Abraham Lincoln and any of the political technicians of his time, or between Albert Schweitzer and his now-forgotten critics who wondered how a gifted man could "waste himself" on the Africans. Let me explain why this is so, first in a general way, then in more detail.

Reason is utterly necessary to mankind. We are what we are because of our capacity to think—because of the cortical area of the human brain. Civilization could not have been built without reason, nor can it continue to be built in the future without reason. Paradoxically, though, much of the value of reason is its potential for guiding and expressing the enormous power *of the subconscious*. No greater error is made than to think that reason should develop only itself—or, to put it in another way, that if you cannot rationalize or explain an idea factually and analytically, it cannot be accepted as valid.

Let me state the point in an even stronger way. I believe it can be demonstrated that the future of Man rests on the development of the unconscious, irrational, unimaginably deep experience and memory that lie below the level of what we call "reason." This part of our being is of immeasurable importance. It contains countless memories, instincts, perceptions—and many things we do not even know about yet. Our hopes for understanding, organizing, and harnessing the subconscious in a creative way depend on reason. But it is the enormous potential of the subconscious that keeps the role of reason from being sterile.

In one sense, therefore, I take the side of many young revolutionaries and others who reject the contemporary Western obsession with rational thinking. As one poet and teacher writes, "The young, with their poetry reading and Woodstocks, are demanding respect for intuition, emotion, the whole dark and teeming vitality of the archetypal unconscious." [10]

On the other hand, I reject the notion that reason has outlived its usefulness. The attempt to overcome the sterility of reason by shutting out its guiding, controlling disciplines and letting the self express itself "naturally" is a reversion to the primitive. Whatever nobility we have comes through our capacity to reason. Whatever claim we have to lordship on earth is due to our superior capacity to think. We cannot just let nature be. We cannot assume that anything we want to do is all right so long as it comes from "the heart."

In this chapter I shall look at these questions: What evidence do we have that the subconscious exerts a great and pervasive influence on our lives? Why is reason by itself not enough to solve our problems—and worse, even dangerous as a guide? In creative personal and social development, how should we conceive of the relative roles of reason and the subconscious? And finally, what kind of test can a person use to see that his subconscious and reasoning powers are used together when he makes a decision?

Living on the Side of a Volcano

Many years ago I noted a statement in a novel: "Man is like a creature living on the side of the volcano of his unconscious, scratching at its surface with his reason like a peasant tilling his fields." The rest of the novel I have forgotten, but that statement has impressed me as a vivid and accurate description. Interestingly enough, the same analogy is used in the very popular novel by Hannah Green *I Never Promised You a Rose Garden*. Deborah, the young girl with the severe emotional problem, says about her sister: "I never gave her symptoms. The illness is the volcano; she will have to decorate the slopes herself." [11] In other words, reason can do little more than decorate the volcano of the unconscious.

Until recently, in anthropological terms, the human ancestor was without any kind of self-consciousness. For a million years or more (anthropologists are still finding out about this) he did not operate in the way that Man does. He subsisted without a man-size cortex, which is the part of the brain that makes objective, rational thinking possible. Even a chicken has a pinpoint-size cortex. The addition of a large cortex and spinal column produced *Homo sapiens.* They gave him the ability to see himself as a separate subject from other beings, which apparently other creatures cannot do (at least, not nearly so well or perceptively as Man can). While Man's capacity for objective thinking, testing, and experimentation has improved since the times of Plato and Aristotle, his capacity for abstract thought has not.

This relative newcomer, the rational mind, might be compared to a light shining on a volcano, with the dark interior of the volcano representing the subconscious. The light is growing, as a rising sun grows at dawn, but most of Man is still in darkness in the depths of the volcano. The knowledge, memory, and habit patterns stored in our subconscious are scarcely illumined yet. In time the light will begin to come down the sides and interior of the volcano, but at present we really can see little about ourselves. We cannot dimly imagine what we may see sometime hence. Even when we get to the high noon of our rational achievement, we will still not be able to peer into many dark, unknown places.

I have been discussing the enormity of the irrational in a general way. Now let me be more personal and specific, for no reader of this page is an exception to this description. Have you ever explored your thinking and attitudes to see how much of them is irrational? It is an interesting exercise. The following questions are just to help you get started.

Are you afraid of the dark? Many people are afraid of it right in their own homes. The fear does not come from facts or objectivity, of course, but from some deeper source. Or are you afraid of height? This is one of my own phobias, and even though I know that it is irrational and have tried to use reason against it, I have been able to subdue it only gradually and to a limited degree. Or do you fear open spaces, or perhaps closed-in spaces? Many intelligent people react violently to being alone on an open plain, and others, to going into a subway or cellar.

Are you afraid of mice or dogs? It doesn't matter how big you are or how strong, if you are in this group. People may sit down with you, counsel you, try to show you the roots of your fear, but it will not do much good. Bats? Even the enlightened congregation at Fountain Street Church stirs and becomes nervous if a bat is caught in the sanctuary. I have many times observed a bat flying there and hoped that nobody else would see it.

Are you afraid of the shame of becoming poor and going hungry? I know people with a great deal of money who worry about the shame of not having enough to eat someday. "Everything may change, you know," they say. "I could lose all my money." But there is not much logic in that, if you think about it. If it did happen, they would be like everyone else, would they not? And so there would be no shame.

Are you jealous of someone else? Jealousy is a common symptom of irrationality. What another person does is no reflection on you whatsoever. It does not change who you are or what you are. Yet there is practically no one who does not feel consumed by jealousy of others on occasions. Sometimes we may have the force of mind to turn off the attitude, but we cannot do it always.

What about your tastes? You may like chicken but not turkey, or you may like cherry ice cream but not strawberry. It took me to the age of forty to be able to swallow an oyster—a pretty simple thing, really. I would talk to myself and reason with myself but still could not do it. Admittedly your body may be allergic to some foods, but that explains only a few of these prejudices. Most of the time, psychologists tell us, our rejection of a food is due to some emotional relationship or association. The cause has nothing to do with the edibility of the food itself.

What about your reactions to color? I know people who possess a violent dislike of pink; others I know have a "passion" for green, or certain shades of rose. Such feelings have no rational basis that we know of.

Do you ever blush when you do not want to, or become jittery, or break out into perspiration on strange occasions? Long before the human brain could make a person react in such a way, the body system produced such behavior. That is what the body is doing in these cases, even though your brain tells you it is illogical. Our bodies and health are in large part determined by causes over which we have no control. When we do exercise control, it is only to suppress the behavior, not dissipate it—and so nature still has its way with us, hurting us physically without our minds being able to protect us.

Do you dislike Jews (or non-Jews), or blacks (or whites)? Prejudices like these are built into us at childhood, usually, before we can deal with them with conscious thought. And they cling to us even though we wrestle with them, knowing they are inherited from some earlier generation or age that possessed reasons to fear that we do not possess now. Just as we think we have overcome the irrational bias, it pops out again in a moment of surprise—and we are shocked to realize it is still there. It has been demonstrated that no white person can grow up in modern American society without developing attitudes of antagonism to blacks, and the same goes for blacks in their feelings about whites. Again, we may *control* the irrational bias with our rational faculties, but we cannot eliminate it that way.

Do you look at the world through the eyes of a Texan or a New Englander? You may have left San Antonio or Boston years ago, and there may be no reason whatever now for you to keep on viewing certain acts or things as "good" while others are "bad." But those built-in attitudes are with you to stay. René Dubos put it nicely:

> A child brought up in Florence is constantly exposed to sights, sounds, and smells characteristic of this beautiful city; his development is conditioned by the stimuli derived from palaces, churches, and parks. He may not be aware of the responses aroused in him by those repeated experiences. But they become part of his biological make-up and render him lastingly different from what he would have become had he developed in London, Paris, or New York.[12]

What about your loves? Can you really explain in an objective, analytical way why you love this woman or man but not that one? Or why one brother or sister is more dear to you than the others? Perhaps no choice affects our lives as much as our choice of loved ones, yet it is based on a chemistry of primordial reactions that is beyond rational comprehension.

One could go on and on describing irrational behavior of this sort. There is virtually no end of it. Each one of us lives on the side of that volcano mentioned earlier. If we do not make ourselves aware of the fact through reason, other events should remind us of it. Our dreams, for example. They bring out fears and hopes in our subconscious, usually in a strange language that only a behavioral scientist can understand; sometimes they transpose conditions from what they are to exactly the opposite because, even in our subconscious, we try to hide from ourselves.

Again, consider the revelations of hypnotism. Under hypnosis· some people have been able to speak languages fluently that they did not know they knew. Another example is extra-sensory perception. Experiments at Duke University seem to have demonstrated that the mind can understand things that are not in its consciousness or presence. This is all a murky area. We cannot understand it, and we can throw out 98 percent of the testimonials as false, but there remains enough evidence to indicate the presence of the most unusual powers in us. It may well be that sometime in the distant future we may be able to converse with one another without spoken words, and to know about happenings far distant from us without being told about them.

The Shallowness and Treachery of Reason

Turning now to our rational powers, we find the opposite situation from that just described. Although we have reasoned how to build cities, transplant hearts, and go to the moon, this faculty is fragile, inadequate, and unreliable in as many ways as the subconscious is deep and irrepressible.

I think we all know this—not in a rational way, perhaps, but in the totality of our understanding. For example, we do not want a doctor (especially an internist or a generalist) who is merely a good technician; we want a physician who can react to us with feelings as well as with technical know-how. Perhaps no profession has suffered so much from the stupidity of trying to apply reason alone as the medical profession has. An engineer dealing with an inanimate object is one thing; a physician dealing with us human beings is another. What is more insulting than being treated as if we were impersonal systems of arteries, valves, flesh, blood, and bones?

Nor will we settle for a family attorney who is just a reasoning person, or for a teacher who acts like a teaching machine in the classroom with our children. We want performing artists, too, to be more than technicians. What is more empty than an opera that is good only as a technical production? Or a tournament golfer who has the personality of a driving machine?

Beyond considerations like these, however, are more serious and profound grounds for distrusting rationality. Let me mention a few of them.

1. *Reason deludes us with false rationalizations.* Liking something for nonrational reasons, we rationalize our attitude in order to explain it to others or to ourselves. For every irrational fear or bias mentioned earlier in this chapter you will hear people giving seemingly logical explanations to justify themselves. "I'm afraid of the dark because of possible attackers," or "I don't like strawberry ice cream because it has seeds in it." But more attacks occur in daylight than at night, and raspberry ice cream (which *is* liked, perhaps) has seeds in it too.

Taken one by one, such delusions may seem quite harmless. But taken together for a large number of likes and dislikes, they create illusions of rational grandeur that can seriously inhibit self-understanding and maturation.

2. *Reason enables us to evade our feelings.* Finding ourselves in difficult positions, we revert to the logical. We build cases to defend ourselves; we become scientific. Thus we save ourselves embarrassment or keep from being hurt. We do this in emotional love relationships, in politics, even in stock market investment. How many stock market analysts explain away a bad sale or buy on the grounds that the "X" factor was not sufficiently accounted for in their formula, thus evading the fact that impulse, bias, or mood influenced them to twist the data a little so the answer would "come out right"? Since we

are more than reasoning creatures, we run a great risk if we ignore the irrational elements in our thinking.

I wonder if this may not be the basic error in Hitler's ideology. Starting from a false premise, the supremacy of the Aryan peoples, he proceeded to work out all the hatred in his mind, unaware that he was expressing emotional biases and thinking all the time that he was being very logical. He sold the German people on his argumentation because reason enabled them, too, to overlook their feelings.

3. *Reason enables us to conceal self-destructive tendencies.* As psychologists have pointed out, all men and women possess a drive to destroy themselves.[13] It is manifested in an endless variety of ways, some small, some big. Most of us dislike facing this reality, and some of us will not face it. If we want to bury it in our subconscious, reason is the tool for doing so.

How many suicide victims never understood their desire to withdraw from life? Not all, perhaps, but certainly many. Among those who kill themselves more slowly with drugs or alcohol, how many are conscious of the drives that impel them? Some are, but most seem to be only dimly conscious of what is happening. The demon mind hides the truth from them, so they do the worst possible things, not knowing why they do them.

At the conclusion of Leo Rosten's novel *Captain Newman, M.D.,* the young narrator describes what he learned in his years of service in an Air Force psychiatric ward during World War II. "In Ward 7, I learned that no despotism is more terrible than the tyranny of neurosis," he says. "No punishment is more pitiless, more harsh and cunning and malevolent, than that which we inflict on ourselves." [14] Suicide, alcohol, and drugs are only the more obvious forms; the subtler, more insidious forms of self-punishment take a less dramatic toll but, in the long run, an equally serious one. If we are unaware of the animal motivations that prompt such behavior, we cannot hope to correct and control it.

Harnessing the Rational and the Irrational

Having damned reason, I now want to put it in the hero's role as far as spirituality is concerned. Reason is our hope for the future in two ways: (1) Only with *better* use of reason can we reduce the errors and shortcomings of reason itself, such as its proneness to excessive rationalization. (2) Reason is our only valid means of illuminating and channeling our powerful subconscious drives.

That animal heritage of our bodies and minds must be understood for what it is, how it came to be, its justification, its influence, its relationship with the cortical area, its importance. We have only begun to understand it with the help of rational analysis—and our knowledge is coming in the nick of time. There was a day when it did not really matter much whether we understood the irrational, for life was simple enough, so that man could get by with unconscious reactions. But that day has passed. No person writing in the field of psychology would fail to confirm that our life in the West has become so self-conscious, involved, and complicated that we cannot proceed unconsciously, simply, or "naturally" anymore without disastrous results.

It is on our rational powers, and only on them, that we can count to learn about our aggressions, if we want to relate ourselves more happily and creatively to family, community, and society. It is on reason that we must count to understand our lusts, hates, "death wishes," and selfishness in order that we may live more satisfying lives.

But there is more to the subconscious than demonic drives, of course. Here is the source also of so many powers that make us human in the finest sense of that term—compassion, empathy, love, nobility, joy, and appreciation of beauty. And so another role of reason is to help us appreciate and express these other powers. Without them life would be a meaningless exercise.

Therefore when the spiritual person has a judgment to make about a book, a painting, a person, or a course of action, I suggest that he ask himself the simple question, *Does it touch me?* I do not present this as a perfect test, for both reason and feelings can be disastrously mistaken—we are twisted by so many forces that we do not really know how to feel cleanly or think clearly. But it is a useful test in that it asks for a reaction based on feeling and thinking *together*.

It is not enough that the object or idea stir one's emotions *or* satisfy a rational requirement. This is why a subjective criterion such as "I like this painting because it is free and easy," or an objective criterion such as "I like that table because it is a Sheraton" are inadequate. Nor is it enough that the object or idea satisfy both counts individually, passing first the test of feeling and then the test of reason, or vice versa. Rather, the spiritual person asks if it cuts through his feelings and thinking, and appeals to a more basic sense in which the rational and irrational cannot be separated. A question such as, Does it touch me? is useful for that purpose.

In sum, the power of the spirit is that it is greater than either reason or feeling alone. It glorifies reason not for itself but for what it can do for the irrational. And it glorifies the irrational not because it is beyond reason but because, illuminated and guided by reason, it can enrich our lives.

In later chapters we will consider various social and political problems our country faces. In every one of them, we will see, our subconscious attitudes are part of both the problem and the solution. Therefore, we cannot understand how these problems developed unless we apply our rational powers. Nor can we see what constructive action is needed until we use reason to check those subconscious forces which aggravate the problem, and to bring forth those instincts which can help us deal with the difficulties.

The Dubious Quality
of Gratitude

Anyone who ever laughed at the antics of Joe E. Lewis, the entertainer, will remember his throaty, raspy voice. Lewis explains that his voice got that way early in his career. He was almost beaten to death by gangsters in Chicago, and his throat was slit. He did not quickly forget how lucky he was to survive. Often he would get out of bed in the morning, wherever he was staying, stumble to the window, pull the curtains aside, and say: "I made it again. I *made* it again."

This is an example of the spirit at work. The spiritual person recognizes that the world does not owe him something (though sometimes he may wish it did). He knows that there is horror and evil in the world; he is aware of destitution and deprivation about him. And *because* of these realizations, not in spite of them, he is grateful—grateful, as Lewis was, for the fact of being alive, for the life of others, for the conditions of life.

I believe that there is no virtue that is more self-rewarding than the virtue of gratitude. This conviction has grown on me during numerous years of counseling, observing, and working with many kinds of people in many types of endeavor. What does gratitude do for a person? It enables him to be joyful on more occasions, to celebrate—and as doctors know, this is good for both body and soul. Gratitude enables a person to be more realistic in perception, to see how much he really has (however little it may be by worldly standards) and how futile it is always to be seeking more power and possessions.

Gratitude will help a man or a woman to check or avoid the self-destructive tendencies mentioned in Chapter 5; the grateful person may risk and lose his life for a cause he believes in, but he is not a likely prospect for suicide. Gratitude enables one to be more responsive (not less, as is sometimes supposed) to the needs of others; the more one rejoices in the beauty of life, the more one will want to preserve what is good in the community and to remove ugliness and destructiveness.

Last but not least, gratitude has a wonderful tendency to grow through use, so that its benign powers expand. I know of no cases where, making an effort to feel grateful, a person has not increased his capacity to experience gratitude thereafter. This "law" applies in times of desperation as well as in more normal situations. *Anne Frank: The Diary of a Young Girl*— that poignant account of a Jewish girl's unquenchable spirit in the face of tragedy and doom—is a well-known case in point, but there are countless others, just as convincing, in everyday life.

In short, gratitude might be called a hidden weapon of the spirit. It is hidden in the sense that much of the world never sees it, never appreciates its extraordinary potential and creativity. In fact, much of the Western world seems to think of gratitude as a "weak" trait, a servile quality that characterizes (or should characterize) the unlucky elements of society but not the strong, self-reliant elements. A little reflection will show, I believe, that just the opposite is the case.

Good and Bad Varieties

To begin, let us define our terms. The word "gratitude" is used in different ways, some of which have no spiritual significance at all.

For instance, the "grateful spirit" of thanksgiving that people sometimes refer to may actually be quite destructive of the spirit. This is the case when thanks go to God for, let us say, the fine qualities we think we possess. Gratefulness of this type follows the pattern of ancient peoples who thanked their gods for their conquests in battle, the advent of a man-child, the fruitfulness of a wife, or a personal victory of some sort. A self-congratulatory quality distinguishes this variety of gratitude; it is not what I consider a spiritual quality.

At other times the spirit of thanksgiving has been characterized by recognition of the dependence of the community on the individual, and vice versa. Here there may be more spirituality. When the harvest was brought in, the ancients expressed their gratitude to their gods (and thus the Hebrews thanked Yahweh) by offering some of the crops in sacrifice. When Jesus' disciples saw him transfigured on the mountaintop and speaking with some of the prophets who had been, they wanted to express their gratitude by building three tabernacles. The first Thanksgiving of the Pilgrim Fathers is a beautiful symbol of thankfulness, for the whole destiny of the community was involved. They had come through the first season and were approaching what they knew would be a bitter winter. They thanked God for the harvest and their full barns.

Even in such acts as these, however, the expression of gratitude *may* fall short of the definition I have in mind. The thanksgivers *may* simply be saying, "God has provided in the past, he provides in the present, and he will provide in the future." Or they *may* be trying to cajole God into blessing them in the future by acting so grateful for what he has done for them in the past. This is a subtle form of bribery. Unfortunately it is common. So often gratitude arises in times when achievement is threatened, or when grave perils have just been surmounted and it is feared disaster may strike again. In such cases thankfulness is not always offered with the ulterior motive of winning God's help in the future, I realize, but certainly that is frequently the reason. And when it is, thankfulness is not an expression of spirituality but an obstacle to it; God and the world are seen as objects to manipulate.

To generalize, it seems to me that those forms of gratitude which are selfish or arrogant are "bad." They are selfish if the purpose is to protect a person's physical interests, as in the examples just given. They are arrogant if the person offering thanks assumes that God's hand is on his shoulder, guiding him in person. "Somebody up there likes me," we say, meaning (unless the slogan is said in jest) that we rate a special relationship with God because of who we are. Such forms are "bad" in spiritual terms because they violate the thinking part of the thinking-feeling function. There is no objective evidence that God can be manipulated or that any group of people or any faith is so good in the eyes of God as to rate special attention.

What about "good" gratitude then? It might be defined as a feeling of wonder that one lives and can experience life. It is awareness of the abundance in the world, of creativity. When a person has such awareness, he sees; and if he sees, he is grateful. Gratitude is recognizing that we get far more than we deserve, even the poorest of us. Whatever satisfactions we experience, we have not created them. We may have paid for them, but we did not create our capacities to enjoy them, nor the hands with which we may have earned them, nor the other hands and natural resources that brought the things of satisfaction into existence.

To define "good" gratitude in another way, the more universal the things we are grateful for—that is, the more they belong to everyone (such as life does, or a beautiful day)—the more spiritual is our gratitude. Conversely, the more our gratitude is for physical possessions, like comfort and money, the less spiritual it is.

For example, the gratitude of Francis of Assisi is very spiritual. In his "Canticle of the Sun" he expresses gratitude not for his mind, his riches, or his good luck, but for the things that belong to everyone: the sun, the moon, the stars, the wind and weather "by which thou [the Lord] upholdest life in all creatures," water, "our brother fire," the earth and its vegetation, people "who pardon one another for his [the Lord's] love's sake." These things we never lose. This is why spiritual people can express gratitude in the midst of suffering, tragedy, and failure. They have lost none of the universal things. They would agree with William Shakespeare:

> My crown is in my heart, not on my head;
> Not deck'd with diamonds and Indian stones,
> Nor to be seen. My crown is called content.

What's So Wonderful About the World?

"But," some people ask, "is there really that much to be thankful for?" If things are going well, why bother to take time out to be grateful? And if things are going poorly, what is there to be grateful for? They remind me of the story of the man who had a leaky roof. When it rained he couldn't repair it, and when it was not raining there was no need to fix it. When things are going well we feel no need for gratitude, but when all is in jeopardy we look around and wonder what there is to be thankful for!

Why may we find it hard to be grateful? To begin with, we like to think that we do things ourselves, that what we have got, we got by ourselves. "I worked long and hard for what I wanted. I suffered greatly to get it. Nobody gave me anything."

Then, too, there is the ubiquitous fear, especially among the powerful and affluent, that hostile forces may take away from us the fruits of our hard work. No supernatural force exists to check the evil forces of theft and destruction. "God is dead." What reason is there for gratitude in a world where evil seems so often to win and where the possibilities of good are so precarious? "Should I be grateful because I happen to be strong enough or lucky enough to have been in a family or company where abundance existed and I was rewarded for hard effort?"

No wonder that gratitude does not come easily to many of us. Surely many people do labor very hard for the success they have achieved, and certainly the forces of destruction often do have the upper hand.

But there is still another reason for ingratitude—an even stronger one. When we are in the midst of poverty, what is there to be grateful for? Should we be grateful for peace in our city or town when all about us in the world there is no peace? Should we be grateful for our comfort and security on a fine Thanksgiving morning when thousands of young men are dying in a war in Asia or the Near East? Should we be grateful for the good fortune that has attended our children when our friends have lost their children? Should we be grateful for the beautiful world we can see and touch when there are many who cannot see or feel?

Let me try to answer these objections with three observations:

1. *Gratitude is necessary and constructive.* The ultimate validity of any value is necessity. Gratitude is not a luxury or decorative quality but an essential quality to mature, thoughtful living. The grateful person is not insensitive to ugliness and evil but keenly aware of it. Seeing the seamy side of the world, he finds it necessary to see the delightful side too. It is the *whole* that he must see, the good along with the bad, else he must either shut evil out of his mind and become half a person, or put up emotional defenses against evil by becoming bitter and cynical.

In addition, gratitude never destroys, never hurts. And I know of nothing except love that grows so beautifully on itself. When we feel grateful we increase our capacity for gratitude in the future; bear in mind that this quality is a form of seeing and understanding, and once we see the reality, we are better able to see it again (as when we first learn to see a star, or gain practice in recognizing a certain kind of foliage in a forest).

2. *We get much more in life than we deserve.* As indicated earlier, it is an utter illusion to feel that whatever we possess has been earned by our diligence and labor. Once I saw a statement that I have remembered ever since: "Thank God, we do not get only what we deserve." If we possessed only what we can take credit for, what miserable creatures we would be! Our minds and bodies were programmed for us before we were conscious by a creative process we have had nothing to do with; the schools we attended were built by other people; forests we use were seeded from an earlier generation of forests; and so on. In fact, it is difficult to find *anything* that we really can take full credit for ourselves. It is a perfectly obvious fact, yet we go around acting and talking as if we get back from life only what we put into it.

3. *Every one of us has much to be grateful for.* If you are

reading this page, you can see. When you got up this morning, were you glad you could see? No doubt you took it for granted, but your eyes were a gift to you. I know some blind people who are more grateful for their senses than most people I know who can see, probably because they know enough not to take everything for granted. You can see colors through the window, perhaps angry skies or white clouds or autumn foliage, and you can see the faces of your children or friends. You can see selfishness and thoughtlessness among people on the street, but you can also watch a mother take her daughter's hand. The nervous system alone that made that gesture possible contains many scientific mysteries, and the mother did not ask for the system: it was given to her.

Let me offer another everyday illustration. Sometimes after the Sunday morning service people say to me, "You must have found it very difficult to open the service this morning by saying, 'This is the day which the LORD has made.'" Why was it difficult? Because it was raining or dark? When we have so few days in the world, are we to let one be spoiled by clouds? And if you look at it another way, the weather is not even inclement. It is part of the natural balance in an invigorating climate. Although we know that the stormy days are essential to the balance, and come regularly every November and December, they become a cause of complaint to radio announcers and people on the street. We are so familiar with our blessings that we do not even think of them as good!

Once when I was talking with a friend, he looked at a glass of water and said: "I was without fresh cold water for two solid years. I never see a glass of fresh cold water that I do not feel grateful." The deprivation made him aware of his blessings, but the rest of us, not having had such an experience, are too busy with our daily routines and tasks ever to think about it.

Why No One Notices

Most of us will hasten to deny that we are ungrateful. If questioned, we can readily list a number of things we are thankful for. Nevertheless, it is my observation that very few people in this world live gratefully. From time to time gratitude may overwhelm us, but the occasions have to be special—and even then they are not long remembered.

For instance, many of us have found ourselves in desperate situations and said, "Oh, God, if I ever get out of this, I'll never complain again." But how many of us do stop complaining when the crisis is over? And doctors tell me that when a person becomes sick, he or she will vow willingness to do anything, pay any price, to get well again. Two weeks after the operation or treatment the patient may remember nothing about it!

How many people who have had their sight restored by cataract operations feel grateful, a month later, for the shades of color they can see or for the lovely form of a tree they can watch through the window? How many young men who returned from the jaws of death in Vietnam still feel thankful that they escaped? How many of us avoid meeting on the street someone who once helped us out of a scrape?

Such behavior, and our obliviousness in general to gifts and givers, can be attributed to various causes. It is helpful to be aware of these causes if we are to see (later in this chapter) how to cultivate a sense of gratitude.

For one thing, we lose our ability to be grateful because of pride. One of the first sentences learned by one of my children was, "I do it myself." My wife and I used to chuckle about this, and we have often wondered what was the basis for that little girl's pride. Did she feel that she had to prove something to us? Did she feel that she ought to be able to do it herself? Or was this a defense against our smothering her, or maybe a way of drawing attention? In any event, the tendency becomes quite noticeable among adults. We do not like to feel dependent on others; we want to owe nothing. In general, our "do it yourself" culture encourages this attitude. And the more we insist on this stance, priding ourselves on what we have done to get us where we are, the less gratitude we can feel.

Of course, pride is an aspect of insecurity, which is a second cause of obliviousness (note that these and other causes may not be conscious or rational). We do not want to put ourselves in another person's or group's power. Only with control in our own hands do we feel able to trust ourselves. If we are beholden to others, we may even come to resent and despise them. Indeed, no human spirit can afford to be in bondage to another, and gratitude in chains is a bondage of the spirit; the chains are as strong as any steel chain.

Third, we are ungrateful because we are too busy to notice. Busyness is a way of reducing a culture to an animal level where there is no awareness, no self-consciousness, no tenderness, no responsiveness.

A fourth cause is custom, habit, routine. We do not see the buildings we pass by daily simply because of the repetition; we do not see the girl look with adoration at her boyfriend because we have seen that look before.

The desire for comfort and security is another cause of obliviousness to the gifts around us. When disturbances occur, as they must every day, we become so preoccupied with them that we do not notice objects and behavior that might otherwise delight us.

Cynicism is a hindrance to gratitude. If our reaction to help from some person or group is "They did it because they had to" or "They must be trying to buy something," we may be able to justify ingratitude in our minds.

Still another obstacle is an inferiority complex. If we feel inadequate in the competitive struggle, we find it difficult to accept the fact that there are always other people who are more talented, energetic, or fortunate than we are. In the effort to prove we are as good as anyone, we become arrogant, brash, insensitive. In competition these qualities might be called pseudo strengths because sometimes they give us an advantage, but of course they are not real strengths, at least, in reaching toward a richer, more satisfying life.

Finally, what might be called "theological shyness" is an important cause of obliviousness to the everyday gifts we receive. Traditionally, most religious groups in the United States and other nations of the West have taught that rewards are bestowed on man as a result of God's favoritism. Explicitly or implicitly, the various interpreters of the Christian faith have generally assumed that God looks after a good person and, either in this life or the next, provides him with abundance. But today there is a noticeable breaking away from this venerable concept of an anthropomorphic God; people of all faiths find it increasingly difficult to accept. Not wanting to be found guilty of retaining an outmoded religion, they hesitate to say in any way, "Thank you, God, for all the gifts that we enjoy but have not earned."

In short, unacceptable forms of religious training in childhood have produced a mood and an environment in which gratitude is soft-pedaled. Our children are growing up in societies that do not encourage them to look beyond their own abilities for the source of countless benefits and satisfactions.

The Art of Counting Blessings

Rarely is a person born with a keen sense of gratitude. Perhaps only the saints possess it as a natural gift. Most of us have to learn to be grateful and keep training ourselves to be appreciative. Our desire may spring from witnessing the poverty of people who have plenty, from a determination no longer to endure the miseries of ingratitude, or from a vision of a better life.

How do people develop a sense of gratitude? Having watched many individuals do it, I want to indicate some principles that were helpful to them and should be helpful to others. These principles reflect a number of observations made earlier and serve as a kind of summary description of how a grateful American might think.

1. *Gratitude comes by stopping to think about it.* If we wait for gratitude to come to us, in all likelihood it will never come. To develop the attitude, a person must seek it. This means pausing every so often during the daily rush to get things done—the pauses need not be long—and simply reflecting on how much there is to be grateful for. Any of the senses of sight, hearing, smell, taste, and touch can be used.

If this effort is made, gratitude will surely come. Indeed, this is where the Biblical injunction, "Seek, and you will find," applies with full force. That injunction does not apply to the pursuit of popularity, power, affluence, and other such matters, but it is 100 percent true in the case of gratitude.

2. *The everyday and most apparent gifts are good ones to notice first.* For instance, it helps to begin by reflecting simply on the gift of human life. Grateful people pause often to marvel at the fact that they are life come to consciousness —or more marvelous still, that they are made of the same energy of which a chair, tree, or earth is made, only they are made in a form that enables them to understand, wonder, and analyze. And they will marvel at common aspects of nature such as the growth of a seed or the intuition of an animal.

3. *Gratitude grows with the realization that the world owes us nothing.* Grateful people do not damn the weather because

it is cold or raining, nor do they become cynical if they do not gain the positions or security they may be thought to "deserve." They realize that the cold and the rain serve a purpose—if not theirs, nature's. They realize that failure to achieve somehow serves an ancient civilization-building process (think what the world would be like if everyone got what he worked for!). In short, they accept that the world is not made for them.

Now, this goes against the grain as far as many people are concerned. We are used to thinking about the rights of people, the obligations of society to the individual, guaranteed minimum standards of living, and similar responsibilities. We Americans in particular have got into the habit of thinking that each child is born into the world with certain claims on society, regardless of color, sex, and creed. This is as it should be, but let us not forget that these are artificially created rights and obligations.

In naked reality, no one is born with a promise that he will be able to see, feed himself, or live out a certain number of years. He has absolutely no claims on nature, God, man, or anything else. He possesses no God-given assurance even that life will go on; the fact that it has gone on all through history obviously does not mean that it must continue that way forever.

In the view of some people, this reality might be cause for bitterness or chagrin. But of course that would be an irrational response, since bitterness can be justified only if one might reasonably expect otherwise—and in this case no such expectation can be supported since the situation was never otherwise. It has *always* been this way.

And so the spiritual American is grateful for every aspect of life that he can see, hear, smell, taste, touch, or know about. And he is grateful for the senses he can use, grateful if he is not hungry, grateful just that he lives at this moment, with no promise of a tomorrow. The more he realizes that life is a hazardous adventure on a small planet on the outskirts of a great galaxy, of which there are millions, the more he tries to keep any hour from slipping by without gratitude for the gifts that make the experience possible.

4. *Deprivation and loss make the learning more profound.* Although gratitude does not require that we experience misfortune, it develops faster and more fully when we suffer losses or the threat of loss. A person who has not lain in a bed from which he cannot rise may be slow to appreciate the capacity to sit up and walk; the person who has not lived under a dictatorship may be slow to appreciate freedom; a person who has not felt hate in his heart may be slow to marvel at his capacity also for compassion.

5. *Any victory is worth celebrating.* Some of the most distracting times I have experienced have been conferences with people in despair. I have seen them sitting in the midst of victories but not seeing their accomplishments. When I pointed this out, the reaction to a victory would be, "Oh, that's nothing."

People acquire gratitude by delighting in their own and other people's achievements, especially achievements that have not been won in competition or at the expense of someone else. Noncompetitive, nonquantitative victories are victories of mankind, and it does not matter whether they are common or unusual. A child's drawing is as much cause for rejoicing as a space-age feat.

The grateful person does not "play it cool" in the sense of acting unimpressed with ordinary accomplishments. In celebrating them from time to time, he finds a way of breaking the workaday tedium, relieving boredom, relaxing tension, and renewing his capacity to respond to problems in fresh ways.

6. *The spiritual person always has enough.* He realizes that if he does not have enough now, he never will. One person can be more grateful for a single friend than another person is for a thousand house guests. One person can be grateful for a piece of bread and a glass of water, while another can writhe in resentment at a banquet table.

And the grateful person always gets more. I have never seen a person who was grateful for having enough who did not get more. The contrast between this rule and the laws of materialism is so stark that many of us find it hard to believe, yet I am convinced that anyone can confirm it by trying it. For instance, gratefulness for what capacity a person has to love will surely lead to his becoming aware tomorrow of more ability to love; and if he feels grateful for friendship today, he will find more friendship tomorrow.

The other side of the coin, as I tell people, is that "if you don't have it today, you never will." For instance, if a person sees no miracles in life today, he will not see them tomorrow; if he sees little to be grateful for in the behavior of friends today, he will not see more to be grateful for when tomorrow comes.

In the world of competition and acquisition, of course, just the opposite is the case. For instance, the feeling of well-being about my financial status today may disappear dramatically tomorrow when some unexpected bills come in the mail. (This kind of experience is so well known that many people refuse, out of superstition, ever to admit that their finances look good or that a project seems to be going well.) On the other side, a belief that one does not have enough power today may motivate him to get more power and consolidate it successfully tomorrow (though he may feel as insecure as ever).

Floyd Patterson Revisited

It is difficult to overemphasize the importance of gratitude. It comes closer than any other quality I know of to describing the spiritual person. It has an endlessness about it: the last minutes of a grateful person are as beautiful, if he is conscious, as the minutes at birth or in the prime of life. Gratitude can make a wondrous thing out of a simple, ordinary life. It could work wonders for America.

Does it stop people from activity and vigorous involvement with business, government, community, and church affairs? Of course not. Gratefulness makes people more productive and creative, not less. They do not crawl into their shells when defeated in competition. They do not seethe with resentment over the course of affairs with which they are concerned, taking their frustration out on themselves or their families. They do not go stale because of boredom; as experts on creativity have long told us, the qualities of wonder and awe are powerful stimulators of inventiveness.

But it also must be emphasized that the price of gratitude is the need to work at it continually. The six principles described do not eliminate the sources of ingratitude that were mentioned; they do not lead to the disappearance of pride, feelings of inferiority, insecurity, and the rest. Those qualities stay with us and may produce ingratitude at any time. The distinguishing characteristic of what I call the grateful person is not that he is never ungrateful—only a saint can be characterized that way—but that gratitude is important in his outlook and is ever growing in importance.

In Chapter 2 I mentioned the tragedy of Floyd Patterson, who had wealth, friends, and fame but was dissatisfied with what life had brought him and was waiting, training, concentrating his thoughts on another chance to prove himself. Yet this same man, about five years earlier, had been well aware of his blessings. "All my life I have been running and running to get somewhere," he had confided to a reporter at the earlier time (he had just won the heavyweight championship), "and then finally one day I woke up and realized how stupid I was, for I was already there."

The story has two morals. First, a person's gratitude can disappear abruptly if it is the result of material victories. Second, only the *practice* of counting blessings can be guaranteed to increase awareness of them. Beyond their implications for individual happiness, both points are crucial, as we shall see later, to an understanding of the American Dream.

"Kilroy Was Here"

One of the most important qualities of the spirit is that it squanders. To anyone who has been brought up (as I was) in the aura of the Protestant ethic, "squandering" has bad connotations. It was not by squandering that American civilization was built, we are told, but by industry, thrift, and sobriety. I will not argue with that.

Yet I am convinced that one of the "secrets" of spirituality, so to speak, is its prodigality. It spends more than it saves. It appreciates more than it accomplishes. It values being more than doing. While it respects the Horatio Alger ideal, it sees it only as a means to a limited end. And *because* of these qualities, not in spite of them, the spirit grows in strength, vitality, and creativity.

To explain why this is so, we need to turn to a question that practically every thoughtful person has wrestled with: How do I face the fact that I won't live forever? We feel that life is a precious gift, so wonderful that it is impossible for any one of us to understand the prospect or necessity of our death. We know in our minds that it will happen, and we rationalize it, but the loss is too much to comprehend in a profound way. For most of us, there is such a horror associated with death that we go through life refusing to face the prospect. We may even devise ingenious schemes of fooling ourselves into thinking that the day can be postponed somehow. For instance, a leading student of Wall Street suggests that estate-building is, for many people, a subconscious method of trying to defeat death.[15]

The desire for immortality is practically universal. When we are children, we write our names on walls and signs; later we carve our initials on trees and benches; and in adulthood we put our names in documents and, sometimes, on books, wall plaques, cornerstones of buildings. What we are really saying is: "I am here. I want you to see me. I don't want to think I can go through life with nobody knowing or caring."

In the end, when we put our names on stones over where our bodies are laid to rest, the notion is: "Don't forget me. My life was meaningful and important."

During World War II, countless U.S. servicemen wrote the slogan "Kilroy Was Here" on walls, stones, and buildings wherever the troops went. It was a way of expressing the importance of their lives; they were not going to get lost in the jungles or buried in the mud somewhere without it being known that they had passed that way first. My psychologist friend, Dr. Irving Goldaber, has pointed out to me that the slogan also served as an assurance of survival. When servicemen came to places of danger and found the statement scrawled on walls, it was a reminder that others had come by earlier and survived. It gave them a sense of confidence that they too could risk their lives and survive. In a scene in one of the postwar movies, a soldier jumps into a precarious shelter, with the hail of destruction all about him. As he huddles in fear, his eye catches sight of the words "Kilroy Was Here" scrawled on some bricks beside him. The words give him hope.

Now, how do we deal with the fact that our days are numbered? Or, more generally, how do we approach the threat of losing things that are very precious to us? With this question the differences begin. There are two basic approaches to an answer. (Each has its variations, of course, but we need not describe them here.)

Pie in the Sky

First, we can hoard. We can hold on tightly to what we cherish—and the more threatened we are, the tighter we can hold on. Money, property, children, status symbols, and other objects are stored in one manner or another as if, by making sure of their preservation, the life of the person can itself be preserved. It is a sad commentary that many older people behave in this way. With so few years to live, they become ever more desperate about holding on, dispensing even with their previous generosity and charity.

Of course, as the conventional wisdom recognizes, "You can't take it with you." It is more important to recognize the destructive effect that hoarding has on our emotions and human relationships. There is an old parable about a man who wanted very much to possess a certain bird. When he finally caught it, after years of trying, he held it so tight that he killed it.

Hoarding is apparent in many ways in American life. In fact, it is the prevailing philosophy in affluent, industrialized societies. As a way of life it means preparation, saving, putting off today until tomorrow. We are a restless people. We are always running. We are always stocking up for the future. "I'll travel when I get enough money so that I can do it comfortably," we say. Or, "I'm going to enjoy myself when I get away from the family and get into college." We rush through the morning to get to the golf course at two o'clock, and while playing in the foursome we are secretly waiting to get back to the bar. We go to the theater and spend much time thinking about the party afterward we want to attend. We spend months planning a trip to Europe; then as we go through Belgium we are looking ahead to Germany, and in Germany our thoughts are on reservations and sights to see in Italy. Another day, another place. Almost never is it now.

One of the saddest things of all is the lengths we go to to prepare ourselves for college, jobs, marriage, children, power, and the rest. How often the much-planned-for tomorrow never comes! Or worse, it comes but it is empty. Then comes bitterness and the futile thinking back—and sometimes the tragedy of the middle-aged person trying to live his youth over again.

If hoarding is so ill-fated, why do we keep doing it? Let me mention a few reasons:

1. *Ability to plan.* Memory, imagination, and the ability to look ahead are qualities that make humanity and society possible. As civilization becomes more complex, these qualities become increasingly important. But as is so often the case, our strength is also a weakness. For many of us the capacity to foresee becomes more than a means to an end; it becomes an obsessing exercise.

2. *Divine discontent.* We discern that however good life may be, it can be better. We sense that we are finite creatures living in the infinite, that the achievements of today are only suggestive of what can be attained tomorrow, that the great knowledge possessed by man today is only the beginning. Here again is a wonderful insight; the saints have possessed it just as other men have. The trouble comes from magnification of the quality by our Judeo-Christian tradition, especially those parts tending toward the Calvinist and Puritanical. We come to feel that it is unwise or immoral to be happy. "I feel so guilty when I feel right," people have confided in me. We

reject compliments. "It was nothing," we say, or "Anyone could have done it." Many people restrain themselves in celebration of a victory with such notions as "Pride precedeth the fall."

3. *Materialism.* Our genius in the West has been our ability to manipulate money, manpower, materials, and other resources to serve the goals of a higher living standard. We train ourselves in apprenticeship. We invest today's earnings in research for the future, or we forgo current income "so that we can expand next year." This is a wonderful and precious capacity of man—at least, until the wealth-building process it serves becomes a way of life.

4. *Future salvation.* Years ago there was the song "There'll Be Pie in the Sky When You Die, Bye and Bye." It was a satirical reflection on religious zealots who would satisfy discontented people by assuring them that their neglect and impoverishment would be made up to them in the hereafter. "Never mind this world, there's another and better one coming."

Today, even in the more traditional, conservative Christian faiths, such assurances tend to be taken at less than face value —more poetically, perhaps, than literally. Still, the notion that there is something more than this life is a prevalent one in our culture. It is an insight that cannot be dismissed simply because of the lack of scientific evidence. What is troublesome is the tendency, evident today just as during the religious heydays of past centuries, to *neglect* or *sacrifice* the potentials for joy in this world because of belief in a better world to come.

Growth by Squandering

There is a second way to approach the question of temporary pleasures and lifetimes. This is to use possessions with joy and a sense of abandon. Whether the possession is life itself or money, the idea is to spend it, make the most of it.

One example that occurs to me comes from the great depression of several decades ago (the recent recession afforded similar examples). I remember several cases of people who had been very hungry, standing on the edge of subsistence and just barely able to eke out an existence if they watched every penny (and I mean that literally), suddenly coming into a windfall of, say, a few dollars. What did they do with the money? They would "blow" it on a party. They did not stash it away for future emergencies, they used it in celebration!

I observed such incidents with awe. They were hard for most of us to comprehend. One observation helped me to understand later on: most of those who were able to "let it go" in this fashion were people who had been to the abyss of utter poverty and knew what it felt like. They had not liked it, *but they were no longer in terror of it.*

I believe that a fundamental aspect of human nature is represented in that behavior. Similar examples can be found in the experience of primitive tribes. A group will go hungry for months, finally make a big kill, and have a wild party of celebration. There is no thought of hoarding. I am aware that sometimes such behavior manifests psychological disease, but on the whole I consider it evidence of an important quality of the spirit. The person says: "This is my windfall, I'm going to enjoy it. I will not be frightened by the thought of not having it later."

The same attitude was taken by many religious saints. Adventurers for God, they went to deserts, jungles, leper colonies, and other danger zones, risking life and investment—their whole capital—without any means of hedging their bets and holding something back in reserve. "This is my adventure, my mission, and I'm going to live it in full." If they could have hedged the risk in some way, the sense of spending themselves, the feeling of commitment, would have died within. That is another way of saying the spirit would have died.

From the standpoint of the Calvinist, the Puritan, and the doctrinaire capitalist, the squandering approach is appalling. It is uneconomic. It is indeed all those things—*if* one proceeds on the assumption that somehow life can be conserved like material capital.

The Calvinist might also accuse the spirit of being hedonist. While there may appear to be a similarity, it is superficial. Hedonism connotes living today to the hilt for the sake of sensuous pleasure. The hedonist would be happy to join the spiritual person in a party of celebration but not to risk physical pleasure for the sake of emotional adventure or a sense of commitment to an exciting cause.

Let me describe the spiritual approach in terms of its attitude toward time: Every minute is seen as a minute to use or lose. No one knows that he will have a tomorrow; this moment, this hour may be the last. It is a frightening thought to some people, but to spiritual people, like any fact, it is as thrilling and significant as one wants to make it. Just as this hour cannot be saved, so the spirit cannot be saved. Nor can it be stored up; there is no place to put it. But the spirit will be greater tomorrow if used today. The more it is used, the greater it will be. In this respect it is like muscles and memory, which also grow through use and atrophy with disuse.

I remember a magazine article containing a reminiscence by a professional writer. One evening while a fire crackled in the fireplace of his study, he was working, as he often did, on an article to be published five or six months hence. With the additional income and prestige the article would give him, he thought, he would be able to spend more time away from his study and with the children. All of a sudden he woke up to the fact that the time for that pleasure was not five or six months hence but right then. Downstairs the two older children were laughing in front of the television set, and upstairs his wife was bathing the baby. He stopped his work and went out to join them. "It's now or never," he realized, "for tomorrow never comes."

To Do or . . .

Related to the two approaches just described are two life-styles for carrying them out. For the sake of brevity, I will describe the two as alternatives, whereas in reality a person will emphasize one over the other but not practice it exclusively.

The first life-style, related to the hoarding approach, is to cram the day full of activities—in particular, activities that qualify us for the community "Who's Who" and establish us as important citizens. Ideally, there is never an hour when we are not busy. Even our "vacations" will be scheduled full of visits, cocktail parties, golf games with valued associates, and so forth. Our assumption is that busyness is the measure of the meaningfulness of our lives. With luck, it will enable us to accumulate investments, nice furniture, expensive equipment, local prominence, and the rest—in short, to become successful hoarders.

This life-style, emphasizing *doing*, is so common in the West, and especially in the United States, that every reader will have had firsthand experience with it. Many will have already observed its weakness: sooner or later the doer looks back on his frenetic activity and wonders what happened to life in the living of it. T. S. Eliot has put the problem this way:

> The endless cycle of idea and action,
> Endless invention, endless experiment,
> Brings knowledge of motion, but not of stillness;
> Knowledge of speech, but not of silence;
> Knowledge of words, and ignorance of the Word.
> All our knowledge brings us nearer to our ignorance,

All our ignorance brings us nearer to death,
But nearness to death no nearer to God.
Where is the Life we have lost in living?
Where is the wisdom we have lost in knowledge?
Where is the knowledge we have lost in information? [16]

Again, those who have seen Thornton Wilder's play *Our
Town* will remember the poignant scene when Emily, who has
died in childbirth, is granted her wish in heaven to return to
the family homestead for a few minutes. The setting she enters
is the house running on a typical day when she was a school-
girl, with her mother, Mrs. Webb, bustling about. Emily wants
just to see everyone and take in the sight of them, but Mrs.
Webb is too busy to stop rushing. "Oh, Mama, just look at me
one minute, as though you really saw me," Emily cries.
"Mama, just for a moment we're happy. *Let's look at one
another.*" But of course Mrs. Webb cannot hear her, and with
a sob Emily tells the Stage Manager to put her back in
heaven. "Do any human beings ever realize life while they live
it?—every, every minute?" Emily asks.

To Be?

The alternative life-style emphasizes contemplation and appreciation. The "be-er" may be engaged in many interesting
activities and pursuits; and like the saints who were mentioned earlier, he may live dangerously. Unlike the doer,
however, he gains his satisfaction not from what the activities
accomplish for him but from the visceral sense of involvement
itself.

The be-er does not feel that he has to go to all the countries
in the world to know the fascination and glory of the earth. In
fact, he realizes that he does not have to leave his hometown
or city neighborhood to know the miracles of life. The be-er

does not feel that he has to pile up an unmatched record of personal or team victories; he just needs to win now and then to know what victory feels like. He does not have to have large sums of money to know how good it is to share, enjoy, and spend. He does not have to enjoy intimate sexual relations with a parade of partners in order to know the fascination of sex. He does not have to have children of his own in order to know how wonderful children can be and to possess that sense of continuity with future generations that is so important to us humans.

As the preceding descriptions no doubt suggest, I equate the be-er with the person who is strong in spirit. He does not have to write "Kilroy Was Here" to establish the importance of his life, any more than he has to have a list of organizational affiliations after his name or enjoy special treatment at the bank because he is a large depositor. It is not *his* life that is so precious to him, but life; not *his* children, but children; not *his* victories, but man's.

How does this approach affect a person's life? I believe that it is an important source of vitality and creativity. The reason is that the spiritual person gains a sense of self-respect that the nonspiritual person does not possess—and, equally important, he tends to convey such a sense to others with whom he lives and deals. During recent years psychologists and psychiatrists have talked increasingly about the lack of self-appreciation that plagues so many people. The malady originates in our upbringing. If we did a good job in school or in Scouts, we were praised and complimented—we were told we were fine, lovely children. But if the next day we did not do well in the activities, we were failures. One day we were good, the next we were bad; one day we were beautiful, the next we were ugly. And so we never experienced real love, for approval came as a result of what we did, or of what we appeared to be, rather than as a result of our existence as personalities. Not our lives but our deeds became the basis of self-respect, and it does not take great perceptiveness to learn how fickle and superficial are people's judgments of our deeds.

As we became adults, we began rearing our own children in the same way. And we found love and respect continuing to come from friends and associates in the same manner as when we were children. To mention a very common example, I know of a young man who wrote a book that was received well by reviewers and the public. Suddenly he had many friends! Now that he was moving up the ladder of success, people came to value him! He was no longer a nobody. This type of behavior permeates American society (and many other societies as well, e.g., the Soviet Union). It is no wonder that people never acquire much confidence in themselves, for not everyone can win consistently, and not even the big winners can stay ahead forever. Are we no longer worthwhile, then, because we are no longer in the news, or key members of the school committee, or able to leave a large estate?

To look at the situation in another way, consider the person who is emotionally disturbed. He is not helped by people telling him about all the wonderful things he has done or the wealth he has acquired. That kind of response from doctors and friends is not nearly enough. What helps him is confirmation of his value and importance simply as an individual, as a personality. The ones who assist him are those who say, in effect: "What are you worried about? You are you, a fine person, and we need you, we want you with us. We like you."

Only if we develop self-respect on that basis (as the be-er does), can we feel any permanence about our worth. If we are important because we can love, then it is enough to have loved a few people in our limited ways; for however forgotten and passed by, we belong to love everywhere, since the capacity of others to love comes from the same ancient source as our own. If we are worthy because we care for beauty, it is enough that we know beauty in our neighborhoods, and however small or humble the neighborhood, we belong to people everywhere who delight in the beautiful. If we are significant because we can talk with children, respond to them, and share with them our loves, hopes, problems, and failures, it does not matter whether we have children who are legally our own, for we belong to any and all children with whom we have shared in this manner, and we become part of whatever they do.

In short, if it is our humanity that makes us worthy, nothing can take our worthiness away, for we are human no matter how severe our shortcomings and accomplishments. So long as humanity is important anywhere, it is important in us. Therefore, spirituality is a limitless source of pride, self-esteem, and confidence. This point should be borne in mind later on when we consider such issues as violence in America, the control of technology, and the kind of leadership we try to give the world.

What You Don't Like
Won't Hurt You

How do you live with what you hate? The very question seems to run counter to much of the idealism we have been taught. We are taught to destroy the enemies of our ideals and to have no part of movements that threaten our way of life. Many staunch capitalists feel that it is disloyal to trade or associate in any way with Communists; a neighbor may express his disapproval of the family next door by refusing to talk with them; numerous Protestants refuse to set foot in a Catholic church, even for the wedding of a friend or member of the family (and vice versa). If these examples seem "old hat," then consider the many reported instances of young people who are forming rural communes rather than be "contaminated" by urban life, or who refuse to listen, or let others listen, to a speech by a member of the Establishment. I am not saying that the young people's ideals are wrong. I am merely reminding the reader that disassociation from persons, organizations, or forces considered evil and destructive is not only an old habit among Americans and other people of the West but a very prevalent one in our culture.

Therefore, the spiritual person's belief in coexistence with objects of dislike may not be a popular philosophy in many quarters. Yet I believe it to be a necessary and extremely important point of view for would-be individualists and self-actualizers in our society. It represents a very advanced form of understanding of the relationships that bind life together, and when a person strives to put this viewpoint into practice, his spirit is strengthened and stimulated.

How does a spiritual person think about the problem of living with what he hates? It is not a matter of the "stiff upper lip" or "turning the other cheek." His approach is based on a good deal of self-discipline justified on several grounds.

First, he lives with what he considers evil because he knows that it is not necessarily evil—and if it is, it may not always be. Indeed, he knows that what a person rejects is often the very thing he *needs*. How often it happens that the new job a person hates, the community he dislikes, the neighbors that distress him, or the parents he abhors become, later on, the things he clings to! To mention a few examples:

a. In the Biblical story, Paul started on the road to Damascus with the aim of eliminating Christianity. The new faith seemed to him to be utterly destructive of all he believed to be worthwhile, and his determination to destroy it made him feel self-righteous, pious, and dedicated. Then he was converted, and Christianity became life itself to Paul.

b. The Roman Empire felt toward Christianity exactly as Paul had felt, and likewise set out to eliminate it. Yet Rome ended up by embracing the faith, finding it a source of salvation, and handing it on to a long series of succeeding generations.

c. Those who objected to women's suffrage were convinced that it would destroy the body politic. After the Constitutional amendment was enacted, they learned, first, that it was not nearly so bad as they had thought it was going to be, and, second, that it strengthened the basis of democracy.

d. During the 1930's many businessmen became absolutely

convinced that Social Security, minimum wage laws, and other New Deal legislation would ruin the industrial establishment. Most of those businessmen have long since decided that such acts are now much-needed "props" for the economy.

e. From the time of the Bolshevik Revolution to late in the 1960's, the concept of profit-making by industrial plants and enterprises was abhorrent to the Russian Communists. The word "profit" was forbidden except when used in derogation of capitalist systems. But during the 1960's the Soviets came to recognize the value of comparing an organization's income with its expenses, and by late 1970 the Soviet press was criticizing plants and collectives for their low profitability.

Second, the spirit lives with what it hates because an understanding of evil is essential to an understanding of what is good. To use a current example, those who have tried earnestly to understand the radical, extremist groups in our society have encountered much that is destructive, stupid, and cruel. But they have also, I submit, seen elements of a much-needed creative force—for instance, youthful refusal to submit to outdated institutions, and determination not to live life going through the motions of obedience with an empty, passive, cheerless mind.

Third, the spiritual person knows that he can never eliminate people and forces that threaten his values. He may do away with one threat, but its place will quickly be filled by others. He accepts that this is an imperfect world, that people are sinful and imperfect, and that nothing this side of sainthood can keep him truly fair-minded toward all systems of values. The principle of eliminating people and things considered evil would lead ultimately, if all followed it, to their killing each other off.

Moreover, as any good amateur psychologist knows, elimination of an enemy rarely leaves the victor at peace. For mys-

terious reasons, one's sense of danger is not quieted by liqui-
dation of a foe or rival. This theme occurs repeatedly in
Shakespeare's plays. And an expert observer of the Russian
scene describes it in the case of Stalin. Even after he had
wiped out most of the old Bolsheviks whom he feared, Stalin's
suspicions of almost everyone in power persisted.[17]

Fourth, the spiritual person learns to live with what he
hates because to do otherwise is to set a disastrous example
for others. One of the fundamental tenets of the existentialist
philosophy, going back to Immanuel Kant, is that, stated simply, you must make your decision in a given situation with the
understanding that what you decide is binding on all mankind. It is not a "little" act in a local scene but has universal
and eternal implications. Thus if you take to yourself the right
to destroy what you do not like, you give the same right to
other people; your morality is someone else's immorality, your
piety is someone else's evil, your ideals are someone else's de-
basement.

So when we justify destruction of an enemy on the grounds
of the rightness of our cause, we fall into an old trap. Whatever else he may have been, Hitler believed deeply that his
goals were valid and that those who opposed him should
justly be destroyed. The men of the Spanish Inquisition believed with enormous sincerity in what they were doing—they
tortured men not to destroy them but to save their souls for
God! The early Protestants in New England followed a similar
course in their witch-hunts. In the 1950's, Senator Joseph
McCarthy must have felt the same way in *his* witch-hunts.
And surely the motives of the architects of the Vietnam war
cannot be impugned for a lack of idealism. General West-
moreland's reported determination to "bomb them back to the
Stone Age" was framed in the highest of motives: preservation
of the free world.

The Value of an Enemy

Now, before going on let us ask ourselves a question. Why do we call this approach *spiritual?* Why isn't it just "plain good common sense" and self-awareness of one's imperfections?

Spirituality is different from those qualities, and the difference is an important one. Common sense and self-awareness are sufficient to produce humility. For example, if you have these qualities, you know from experience that you can be wrong, or that your "right answer" to a problem is predicated on certain assumptions reflecting personal values and judgment. (Even a computer can be designed to incorporate a certain amount of humility, as when it produces quantitative answers qualified by margins of possible error.) Following such an approach, you may say to yourself about a person you do not like, "He may act that way because of experiences I do not know about, or perhaps because of something I said to him that I have forgotten about." At the political level, wise statesmen know from long experience that their information may be faulty, and so they refrain from precipitous action for that reason.

But spirituality goes farther than this. It recognizes that even if you could have complete self-awareness and perfect factual information, you would *still* be wrong to impose your beliefs on others or to cut off contact with people you consider evil. For enmity is so basic to life that it probably exists within God himself. The greatest of spiritual leaders have understood this in their efforts to see themselves, mankind, and all life in relationship. They have understood that, limited by our finite minds and imaginations, we Christians do not yet, and perhaps never can, understand how, as Job asked the question in

Biblical times, there can be evil in a world ruled and run by God. Yet from the beginning perceptive people have sensed that, whatever the reason, evil is no stranger in the world. In the myths of all peoples, including Christendom, there is recognition that Satan (or his counterpart) is somehow or other a prince *of the spiritual realm itself.* I am sure that this is what Paul meant when he spoke of "the spiritual hosts of wickedness in the heavenly places" (Eph. 6:12). Somehow Satan was an instrument of God, Paul saw; either Satan was created by God when God made the universe, or he was there and God allowed him to remain. And long before Christianity started, the ancients recognized the same truth—the Zoroastrians, for instance, in their notions about the conflict of light and darkness and about both light and dark being a part of their god.

Theologians have wrestled with the question right down to this day. They see in our world a reflection of the enmity that exists within God himself, an enmity which, as stated in the Bible, will never be ended until man and his life on this planet are done. If you find God to be only friendly, you have not found God at all. (I use the term "God" in the broad sense now; I am not thinking of any Christian concept in particular.) If you know him to be only sweet, solacing, tender, and loving, you do not really know him. Into the man-God relationship is built attack, competition, and demands to the end that someday—not in our time nor in our children's time but at some ultimate time—man will be able to confront himself perceptively enough to understand the dark places in his soul as well as his infinite possibilities.

Let me use an analogy with competition in business. We have learned that one virtue of American capitalism is its stimulation of performance. If a business has no competitor or only one or two poor competitors, its level of output and quality is likely to be low. If it is to produce any portion of the excellence it is capable of, it needs to be challenged. In strong capitalist systems, therefore, government and business have been intelligent enough to seek strong, vigorous competition—and, where there is none, to create it.

Of course, another analogy is with the philosophy of free speech and free thought. The great democracies have understood that only through the constant struggle of one viewpoint against another can there be an emergence of an understanding higher than either one. Thus, an advocate needs a rival. Without one, he would be a lesser person. The same principle applies at the broad level of man's relations with himself and his maker.

The enmities of the world have enormous values to the people involved—*so long as* (and here is the obvious limitation of the analogies given) competing does not lead them to hate. When you hate your enemy you cannot see or understand him.

Thus spirituality goes farther than just "common sense" and "self-awareness" in understanding the need for coexistence. Having this deeper understanding, the prophets of Judaism warned, "Do not destroy the enemy, for he may be the messenger of God"; and Jesus, when he was being destroyed by his enemies, did not seek their destruction but asked that they be forgiven. And only if we possess such a deeper understanding can we, *at the time* of our crises and confrontation with what we consider evil, hope to restrain our tendencies to annihilate or withdraw from contact. In retrospect anyone can see that, yes, President Kennedy's Administration made the right decision when it decided against pressures to annihilate Castro's Cuba, and that President Eisenhower correctly decided to withstand pressures to intervene militarily in Hungary when the Soviet tanks crushed the rebellion. But in the heat of conflict when emotions run high, it is likely not to be enough to possess ordinary qualities of humility. This is when one may need the greater strength of a spiritual approach.

Living Under Tension

Now, I have stated that this approach makes a person stronger and a better self-actualizer. I have inferred that it will help him to avoid going through life achieving (or not achieving) with a perpetual sense of dissatisfaction. Let us go back to that notion now, because it is central to the aim of this book. The reason for taking the spirit seriously is not that it makes you a "better" person or a more moral one, but a happier, "more alive" individual.

How does the spiritual approach to enmity help a person? For one thing, because he accepts the inevitability of tensions and the unsolvability of many problems, he doesn't try to dodge conflict or resolve it in a spurious way. He knows that if he tries to end a source of tension by destroying the enemy or group he hates, he will live in guilt, resentment, and anxiety. He will know some of the miseries Stalin knew, for he cannot do without others.

On the other hand, the spiritual person knows that if he tries to get rid of the tension by giving in to the enemy, that won't help either. If he becomes a martyr, makes himself a model of unselfish behavior, and concedes his interests away, the "self" in him will rise up to cry for its rights. Martyrdom is as spurious a solution as its opposite. In my observation, martyrs are not happy, productive people in this world. The beast in them demands recognition. Pretending otherwise does no good. Perhaps worst of all, because the martyr tries to shut his eyes to the beast, he is completely unprepared to cope with him. He does not see how his frustrated instincts for self-preservation warp his outlook or make him bitter.

Accordingly, the spiritual approach to enmity puts you ahead in the respect that you steer between Scylla and Charybdis. But this is not the only gain. More important, in terms of long-run constructive advantage, is that this approach leads you to find more pride in yourself. You find your attitudes more resilient, you find your viewpoints changing, and you experience progress and growth in your understanding. I like to use the analogy of a sailboat here: A sailboat makes headway against the wind because of the resistance of its sail to the wind. It must not set itself against the wind too much or it will keel over, but neither must it oppose the wind too little, for then it will make no headway. It must set itself on a course of firm but "giving" opposition in order to develop forward motion.

Similarly, those who live with conflicts of ideas and viewpoints, seeking neither to annihilate nor to capitulate but to understand better, are the ones who experience "forward motion" in human experience. The avid Democrat who keeps affable working relationships with avid Republicans, the conservative father who maintains a lively dialogue with his hippie son, the dove who stays open-minded to the reasoning of the hawk vis-à-vis the war in Indochina or the Middle East—these are people who know one good way to self-actualize.

But I don't want to make this process sound easy. It is not. The fact is that when you decide to coexist with rivals you take on a very demanding assignment for yourself. However sound acceptance of tension may be in a philosophical sense, that does not make it easy on the stomach and the emotions. Spiritual people can have ulcers, like anyone else.

To add another somber note to the discussion, bear in mind that the day when the average person could escape the turmoil of the world by going into the sanctuary of a church is over. People used to do this with success. No matter how dreadful the strife and confusion in the workaday world, they could find refuge in the sanctuary, a sense of peace in the conviction that God cared for them and was waiting for them in heaven. Fewer and fewer people can really put their minds at rest in this way anymore, and people like myself have not helped reverse that trend. I worry about this. I fear that the terror which will come over many people when they confront this situation may be beyond our imagination. And I am afraid that modern Christianity will suffer as a result, when the terror becomes widespread. It may be thrown back into its dualistic framework of a hundred years ago in a futile effort to find beliefs for people to hold on to. When that fails, our religion may be discredited altogether. Possibly this is beginning to happen already, as witnessed by the mysticism and occultism that is a fad on some college campuses.

What are some practical, everyday methods of handling the tensions of living with enemies and objects of dislike? Let me describe briefly six approaches that spiritual people I know have employed with good results. People do not find them equally useful—an individual will prefer one or two to others. But having carefully observed numerous people's behavior for many years, I know that at least some of these methods will work.

1. *Recognize that your tensions are normal.* It may not be obvious to you, but it is apparent to anyone in whom people like you confide. The fears that you have—of real or imagined threats to your values, of your reasonable or unreasonable impulses to retaliate, and of other things—are shared by many, many other people. Recognition of this fact invariably helps spiritual people.

2. *Discipline yourself to accept tension.* Living with evil is not a matter of "doin' what comes natur'ly." *Most* of the time

you must use much willpower to live with people, ideas, and conditions that you find disturbing. Once you succeed in this manner a few times, however, you will begin to take pride in the approach. To use a homely example, many of the people who attend the Fountain Street Church in Grand Rapids find themselves repeatedly concerned and disturbed over the points of view expressed. They find that they have had to discipline themselves on occasion to keep coming. But having done that, they begin to find the tension quite acceptable, and they want to continue experiencing it.

3. *Make yourself a part of the solution.* All of us, especially those of us who are middle-aged or older, feel temptations to turn the clock back. Suppose we had done such-and-such instead of what we did actually? Suppose we could restore this condition or that? It is a difficult temptation to resist. I believe that spiritual people find it easier to resist if they try to think of themselves as part of a new solution that is needed to a current problem instead of as part of the problem itself. The future, with its new methods and understandings, then becomes less of an enemy to them. They walk with it as a friend. If they can think, "Go with the young people," so much the better. This does not mean that they concede that the young people are right in everything (obviously that is not true); it means that they recognize that, right or not, the young ride the wave of the future, and the elders intend to ride it with them. The spiritual person says that he will not die looking back.

4. *Find some small, concrete tasks to do.* Plant a tree. Clean up the yard. Pick up some litter on the street. Fix the dry well. The task should be simple, trivial, something you can manage, something you can look at and see that it is done. This technique, which has been found so often to be helpful, tends to be overlooked by intelligent people—perhaps because it is

trivial. It takes a person away for a few moments from the big, universal, terribly complicated problems that concern him.

5. *Do something physical.* Much of the tiredness you feel may be due to tension, and physical exercise is a good way of releasing that tension. I believe that getting angry is a temporary "lifesaver" for many spiritual people too. Even though they are sweet, kindly, gentle souls, there is anger in them, and they do well to get rid of it now and then.

6. *Get away from it all.* The most patient, sincere, saintly person finds that there are times when he has to say "To hell with it," or "I'm sorry, I have no more time for that today," and take off. It may be for a refreshing swim, a party, a wedding, a celebration of some sort—but away from it all, a cause for celebration, with problem-solving put aside. For the spiritual person in particular, the sheer sensual enjoyment of living must not be forgotten.

The spiritual approach to discord and enmity has profound implications for our approach to our problems as a nation. This will become apparent in later chapters when we turn to such questions as the development of new moral codes and national ideals.

Some Tests for Measuring
Spiritual Growth

Having examined the powers of the spirit, let us turn now to
the question of spiritual quality and qualitative change over
time. The quality of the spirit is measured by its growth.
Quality is not measured by stage of development or some
combination of contents, as skills and knowledge are.
Therefore we must find ways to assess our growth and to as-
certain whether or not we are growing.

We grow in spirit through involvement. This we know. The
nature and type of involvement determine the nature of the
spirit and its depth. A person can be involved in something
destructive, and if so, his spirit will be affected differently
from the impact of involvement in a constructive activity.

Can spiritual growth be measured? Of course it can! All
qualities can be measured. Often they cannot be measured
precisely, but usually it does not much matter. When we
build a jet engine, there are parts that must conform to perhaps one ten-thousandth of an inch tolerance. But when we
measure the earth's distance to the sun, a hundred miles here
or there makes no difference, and when we measure spiritual
growth we can get along without any numbers at all. For obviously the spirit is not an exact thing—we are not even sure,
in fact, about some of the aspects we are measuring. If I can

say, "I think I am doing better now—not better than a minute ago, but better than when I was a child," that may be enough. Or it may be sufficient that I can detect a noticeable difference in some aspect of spirituality, a little more progress in the direction of some ideal even though the amount cannot be calibrated.

It is surprisingly and strangely difficult to observe growth—any kind of human growth. Those of us who watch children grow up are amazed from time to time to see objective evidence of the growth that has taken place. For as we go along with children, we do not notice their changing any more than we normally notice the aging of our friends.

If it is difficult to measure a maturing physical thing, how much more difficult it is to measure the growth of the spirit! Yet this must and can be done. If the spirit makes so much difference, we cannot afford to be ignorant of whether it is standing still in us, going downhill, or enlarging itself and developing as it ought.

Surprisingly, we can be without spirit and not be aware of the lack. We may be conscious of pain, discontent, boredom, or a sense of failure; but we may not understand that there is a good chance that these distresses may be related to the spirit. Accordingly, symptoms that *should* drive us to a deeper understanding and awareness of the spirit often, in fact, do not.

The tests of spiritual change or growth that follow are not universally valid. One person's tests are a reflection of his perceptions of his particular needs, weaknesses, strengths, and values. The best he can do is offer criteria that another person may find useful in formulating his own set of measures. There is a common denominator of all cases, though: the quality of one's involvement in human relationships is what we are concerned with. If a person is properly involved, his spirit will grow, whether or not he knows it and thinks about it. If we can use the tests to keep the conditions of our lives receptive to growth through involvement, we will have accomplished the main thing. One day in the future we will suddenly realize that we have reached a new point spiritually, and are in the process of going beyond that point to a farther one.

Let me state these tests in the form of questions that the spiritual person might ask himself.

1. *Have I changed my mind recently?*

This test applies to our most cherished, deeply held convictions as well as to other beliefs and positions we hold. In a rapidly changing world, we must run just to stand still. If we are on ground that is vibrating, moving, jolting, rising, and falling, we had better be moving just to keep upright. A bridge has no stability unless it is flexible. The higher and longer the bridge, and the more difficult the circumstances, the greater is the necessity for flexibility.

Stability is not a fixed and fast thing. It means moving with moving times and conditions in order to keep the values that will be lost if we do not see the changing conditions. Businessmen know this very well. They watch the barometers to see how things are changing so that they can change. Out of the changed condition, they get what they want.

How could it be any other way with the spirit? We must forever bend to find the drift of the wind of God as it changes directions. It is always blowing, always varying. We must watch for it, be sensitive and alert to it, and understand it enough to be able to go with it and use it.

Therefore the spiritual person keeps asking himself questions such as these: Have I changed my mind lately about the quality of music I like best? or about what makes for good art? or about the nature of youth? Have I changed my ideas about how people should dress? or how they should deport themselves? or what kind of hair young people should have? Has there been any change in my views about the nature of the community in which I live? or its most pressing problems? Have my feelings about personal success changed? or about what makes for "manhood" or maturity?

2. Have I any new questions for which I am seeking answers?

Has there been anything new in the last month or year that puzzles me? Has some question arisen for which I have no answer and want to find one? It is characteristic of the spiritual person to find from time to time that old answers no longer satisfy him, and to run into new questions every so often. "I don't know," he finds himself saying. "I haven't thought about that. I'll find out."

Another way of stating this test is that increased awareness is a measure of spiritual growth. A person becomes more conscious of who he is. For example, as he grows more mature in understanding, he wants to know more about where he came from, what his ancestors were like, the nature of their times. He is less and less inclined to accept conditions on their face value—how did they come to be? He looks at the world with more wondering eyes. What makes our problems? How did they arise? Is the way things are the way they have to be? Looking at a person, he sees more than a physical organism. How much compulsion is that person under? How much real freedom does he have? More and more, he notices the details of interconnections in all life. As Wordsworth put it, "The meanest flower that blows can give thoughts that do often lie too deep for tears."

3. Have I any new problems?

No one can go on growing without new problems. Just the very fact that he is a year older makes his problems new. How does he handle his physical incapacity today as compared to yesterday? What about his loss of memory? What about the tiredness and the boredom that creep into his life? What should he do about losing (now or later) authority over his children? And what about the differences he has had with his wife?

But this question is also an involvement test. A person who does not have new problems is not involved in the changing life about him. The fact that the composition of so many cities and communities has changed makes new problems for many Americans. The fact that there are blacks now where there were only whites a month ago makes a new problem for numerous people. The fact that people are still moving out of the cities makes a new problem for many of us. The fact that the Chinese have achieved destructive power capable of destroying cities and possibly nations is a new problem for Americans. The old answers are not necessarily the right answers. For a new problem we may need a new solution.

An important assumption is involved here: A problem is not a sign of defeat and trouble; it is a sign of involvement and potential growth.

4. *Have I some new enthusiasms and interests?*

Have I read a book recently that I am excited about? Have I seen an article that I can't wait to give to my friends? Have I come to see something new and meaningful in an art form that I had not seen before? Have I found something new and interesting in the activities of the community? Is there a cloud on the horizon, however far off, that I am watching with excitement as it develops?

The proper kind of involvement in a constantly shifting, changing world will throw new light on fresh aspects of old things. Conditions become new, even though they have been there forever, when a person sees them for the first time. If we could but develop the eyes to see it well enough, the world would be new for each of us every day of our lives.

5. *Have I any unfinished tasks?*

Our society encourages us to solve, wrap up, and dispose of our problems neatly, putting a string around the package. This is supposed to give us a feeling of virtue for having completed our tasks.

Whatever merit that attitude has in business and house-keeping, it does not go with spirituality. The work of the spirit is never done. *The spirit never stops growing.* If we grow in our thinking-feeling understanding of life about us, as described earlier, we will die with more unfinished tasks than we ever had in our primes; for we know more, we see more, we feel more. And we are more aware of the intricacies of relationships and the urgencies of conditions than we ever were in our youth, when we were busy with so many other things.

If we are involved in the *process* of life, the end of our particular span of years in the community does not mean the end of our life. Because of our understanding, we belong not just to this time and place, not just to these bodies; we belong to a process that is endless. This, I think, is what all the theories of immortality have been trying to say to man: "You are much more than a tidy project, here and gone. You belong, and you will forever belong, and there is nothing that has to do with man that doesn't have to do with you." The simple, oft-repeated, beautifully said statements of ancient poets and artists contain valid insights into the human spirit, and they need to be freshly understood and appreciated.

6. *Have I had any failures or shames recently?*

We cannot be involved in life without suffering failures, for involvement means trying for things that are not but ought to be, and reaching beyond our pat, comfortable levels of achievement. To seek in this way is to experience not only defeat in the usual sense but also *shame*. Therefore, this test also implies asking such questions as: Have I found the blood rushing to my face in shame over what I thought I could be, but am not? over a failure of understanding or of the quality of my spirit? Have I stupidly failed to sense, see, and hear as I could have? Have I felt appalled at how selfish, greedy, or frightened I could be?

Even the jobs we do best will continue to be beyond us if we are spiritually alive and growing. I work harder today at my preaching, I know, than I have ever done in my life; yet I know less and less about what it is, and what it means, and what makes it, because I see more of what ought to be, and could be, and is not. And then there are the failures in the human relationships that we treasure most deeply, the unthinking acts toward relatives and friends that make us feel like hating ourselves. "Where are my values? How could I have done that?"

Such shames, devastating as they may be at the time, are not experiences to run from, but to accept and respect. The fact is that they make us more self-aware, at once both more humble in our humanity and more proud, for against the backdrop of these failures we can appreciate our successes better. Paradoxically, defeats also make us *less* afraid of involvement (at least, if we are normally healthy and well-adjusted). Learning that the world does not come to an end because of a humiliating experience, we become less afraid of the risks of new associations and commitments.

7. *Have I overcome any worries?*

Some concerns are valid and cannot be dismissed, as when our children do not contact us when they should, a friend is in danger or difficulty, or a potential disaster looms. Naturally we worry about them. At the same time, it is in the nature of spirituality to conquer many worries. While we see more problems, are more deeply involved, and therefore are more often chagrined, we do not fret as much as we would if we had less spirit. For if we have been building the kinds of loves, friendships, and community in which we know that we are never alone, we sense that no matter what comes, we can handle it. We grow to understand the shallowness of many of our concerns, and are not bothered by them anymore.

8. *Have I overcome any anger or resentment recently?*

This is a test that many people are likely to find meaningful because it mirrors so many of the negatives and positives of spiritual growth. First, let me emphasize some connotations it does *not* have. It does *not* mean the spiritual person never feels resentful or angry; as we saw earlier (Chapter 8), venting anger from time to time can sometimes be recommended as a device for handling tensions. Furthermore, this test does *not* mean walking away from the conflict of opposing viewpoints, or escaping from the tension of trying to decide what is the best way to go in a difficult situation.

Instead, this test bears on the emotional development that follows from a strong spirit. The individual finds himself less angry at many things because he is more willing to discover that he may be wrong, even in his deepest dedication to a particular point of view or conclusion. He is not so much concerned with *his* pride and *his* victory and *his* reputation. Consequently he finds himself less provoked by the attitudes of "those young people" who disturb us so deeply; by the acts of "those revolutionaries" who make us worry so much; and by the statements of "enemy" employers or political factions. Some people may prefer to think of this test in terms of increased respect for others and ability to work with them. The individual reacts to a quarrel not with a vow to penalize or hurt the other person but with self-inquiry. "I don't like her because she bothers something in me that I'm afraid of or want to protect. Though she's antagonistic to me, she's a person. She's the way she is for the same kinds of reasons that I'm the way I am." And so the other person is not seen as an object to be manipulated, compelled, or removed from the scene. Although perhaps continuing to be a problem and a source of discomfort, she is accepted as someone to talk with, share with, and work with.

Possibly the greatest potential value of an organization is that it can bring together people of diverse interests, values, and viewpoints. It can enable people to live intimately with those with whom they disagree. This is the nature of the kind of community we talk about and try to build, for example, at the Fountain Street Church.

9. *Has something warmed my heart lately?*

If our spirits are growing, we experience new excitements, enthusiasms, poignancies. The occasion may be a letter from an old friend, a kindly word from someone, or an act that demonstrates the capacity of the human being to rise above his selfishness. It may be the concern of a parent for a child, or a friend for a friend—some expression that breaks the bonds of time and place and seems to open a window into eternity. It may be an idea, a book, a piece of music, or a civic movement. The spirit's range of appreciation is infinite.

10. *Have I some new standards?*

As mentioned earlier, a person's tests of growth are a revelation of his needs, interests, and development. Since all these change, as the spirit grows, he must find new tests of his awareness of life.

Spirituality is not an accomplishment. It is a *process*. To come to terms with the spirit is not to settle on one or a series of points, but to grow in understanding and never stop growing. There is an analogy here with the concept of process that has become so important in some fields of physics during the past fifty or so years. In these fields the nature, quality, and direction of change in a substance are more important than the particular state or condition at a point in time. To put it in another way, one's spirit is never perfect (or, in religious terms, one never makes it from a state of "sin" to a state of "grace"— one is never "saved" once and for all). If perfection were possible, the implication would be that creativity has stopped, the world has ceased changing. And that cannot be in the world as we know it.

Part III
IDENTITY AND MORALITY

The Deficiency
of Masculinity

With an appreciation of the nature and power of the spirit, it
is not so difficult to understand the malaise of America as described in Part I. Our most serious problem is not external obstacles, such as inflation, urban decay, or international violence (though such problems are real indeed). Nor is it
inadequacies in our talents, knowledge, or skills. It is our perception. In this series of chapters let us consider the ways we
regard ourselves, the roles we try to play, and the standards
we set for social behavior.

We live in what psychologist David McClelland calls "the
achieving society." [18] Our parents gave this culture to us, and
we give it to our children. It is commonly given credit for our
extraordinary accomplishments in gross national product,
technology, and education. Yet, for all its virtues, it has produced a kind of hypnosis that leads us to deceive ourselves
purposely lest we come to terms with the emptiness of our
existence.

Let me illustrate with an everyday example: One of the best
ways to make somebody angry with you is to bring into question the self-improvement ideals of his family or of his organization. If the person is one of those dedicated to "winning" in
sports, law, politics, or the "game of life," the question might

be whether winning is really so important, since you cannot go on winning forever—and when finally you are defeated, what have you left? Or if the person is a corporation executive from a growth company dedicated to the principle of annual growth of 15 percent or 20 percent (or more), then the question might be whether it is really desirable or possible to keep on growing indefinitely at that rate.

Ask questions such as these and you are likely to stir up antagonism. The achievement motive is so bred into us from prekindergarten years on that we can hardly talk about it. We don't like to question the necessity or value of wanting. We become defensive when others question this ideal. If what we have is good, we tell ourselves, then more will be better. "I was always telling my three sons," an industrial leader told a reporter, "that if they marry, marry to strengthen the family." [19] This man was head of a large, prominent holding company in Chicago, but the power and affluence that he had already brought his family were obviously not enough; the family must grow stronger still. What is more, we look with disdain on the person who, ceasing to want more, walks away from the competition of the world with the attitude, Why should I bother about such things?

Our chronic discontent in America is due also to the influence of quantitative thinking. We tend to set our sights on additional quantities rather than on further qualities. Whereas improvements in the quality of life are difficult to assess, it is comparatively easy to set as our target twenty thousand dollars more in savings, or one million dollars in life insurance sales, or a "winning year." Also, quantity of effort is an easier standard than quality of effort; it makes for less strain on our emotions, less anxiety, less uncertainty.

Lewis Mumford is one of those who put great store in this explanation of our social malaise. The postulates of our quantitative, technically-minded society, he states, can be summarized as follows: "There is only one efficient speed, *faster;* only one attractive destination, *farther away;* only one desirable size, *bigger;* only one rational quantitative goal, *more.*" [20]

Now, when we want, we are involved; and when we are involved, we are concerned. We are doing something, we are alive, we are alert. So wanting performs a valuable function; its effect is such as to help us achieve our needs. The trouble comes from forgetting the purpose of meeting a need: increasing the capacity to enjoy life. For most people in the West, this capacity was gained years ago.

For most of us Americans it is fair to state that if we do not enjoy what we now have, we will not enjoy more by gaining more worldly status and possessions. I know of no rule that is more generally true than this one, and I find that most people know perfectly well in their hearts that it applies to them. The problem is that there seems to be no good alternative to wanting to get ahead or acquire more. How else can we find excitement? Unless we are striving and competing for more, how can we feel really alive? Sportsmen often say that it is not the actual winning that is so satisfying, but the effort of trying to win. We do not have an approach to life that gives that pleasure *and also* enjoyment when the things desired are possessed.

"B" and "D" Approaches to Life

The American discontent has roots that go still deeper than the explanations just offered. Let us turn to a third cause. Although an understanding of this cause requires us to step back from immediate problems for a moment and look at the underlying structure of our philosophies, the effort can be rewarding. It will help us to see why some traditional American notions have been getting us into absurd situations.

We do not need to go into the theory in detail. We can begin simply with the observation that there are two kinds of structure in the world.

1. *Mechanical, logical,* and *mathematical* structures are made by technicians, analysts, organizational builders, and society in general. The distinguishing aspect of these structures is their parts: every part is replaceable and functions in a mechanical way with the other parts. If one part breaks down, it does no injury to another part except under unusual circumstances. While the structure as a whole is dependent upon the parts being in working relationship, no one part makes any vital change or impact upon another part except in a functional way.

For instance, the accounting function in a factory is essential if the buying and personnel functions are to perform properly, but internal changes in the accounting group do not affect buyers and personnel people. Similarly, the air-conditioning units in a store must operate properly or the lighting system will add too much heat during hot summer months, but the architects do not need to worry about any other relationship between lighting and cooling. If the first air-conditioning unit fails and different machines are substituted, the lighting system is unaffected and continues to do what it is supposed to do.

Of course, I have simply been describing the way all man-made structures work. Unfortunately we may forget that this is but one way to function—not the only way. The important characteristic of mechanical, logical structures is that they have no time of their own. We can build them slowly or quickly, depending on how much time and ambition we have. They are created and maintained to serve *our* needs.

2. A quite different type of structure is the *organic* system. This type grows at its own rate, according to an internally set

pattern and time schedule. It is dependent upon the environment for growth; it is also dependent upon a far more sophisticated relationship of its parts (if you can call them parts) than mechanical systems are. If one thing goes wrong anywhere, the whole organism may be totally destroyed. Accordingly, organic structures are not readily manipulated so they will grow faster or in certain ways. They must have their own way, grow at their own pace. We can retard their growth by putting obstacles in their environment, or enhance their growth by removing obstacles, but except under unusual circumstances we cannot "hurry them along." It takes so many months for the womb to produce a child, so many years to grow a mature elm tree—and the time has been constant throughout human history.

Here too, of course, I have simply described the way all living, organic structures grow.

Now let me make a second set of observations. These pertain to two kinds of perception that people have.

1. As Abraham H. Maslow points out in his book *Toward a Psychology of Being*,[21] most of us approach the world with our thinking dominated by needs, ideas, hopes, and expectations. Maslow calls this "D-cognition" or "Deficiency" perception. We can get back from life what we want from it, and if we make the right demands, we may become very successful. Moreover, this practical, logical approach to the world is efficient; it is responsible for our technology, transportation systems, cities, medical progress, and high standard of living in general.

Why then is this approach referred to as Deficiency perception or D-cognition? Not because it is ineffective in procuring the rewards we seek, and certainly not because it is dispensable, but because it restricts us from seeing life as it really is. We say, "This man is an Italian," and we go on to understand

him with that knowledge. And so what we see is an "Italian,"
not a human being. Whatever our knowledge of an "Italian,"
whether it suggests wonderful music, Olivetti machines, or
affiliation with the Mafia, it circumscribes what we can see in
that person. Again, we say, "I want a nice family and a secure
job." And so what we get if we approach the task efficiently
and with luck is just that. We never see wonders of existence
that are unconnected with a "nice" family or job security.

2. Another approach to life Maslow calls "B-cognition" or
"Being" perception. The B approach is an effort to see the
whole being—what the Gestalt psychologist calls foreground
and background. Naturally, we still have to see through the
knowledge and values we have acquired, but we try to see
more than that—everything that is there, whether it is what
we meant to see or not.

The B approach can also be distinguished in that it does not
lead us to predetermine or precategorize as the D approach
does. The B approach draws from and comes from the unconscious. It flows from perceptions beneath the level of the rational, scheming, planning, organizing mind. And so things are
seen and felt in a more dreamlike way, not so sharply and
clearly outlined. But more of the whole is seen, more of reality
is sensed.

Psychologists like Maslow believe that only the person with
Being perception is capable of real love. For that person has
the capacity to regress into childhood and infancy, into
depths of intuition created by many millennia of ancestral development. The B approach to love does not see the utility of
the other person; it does not weigh or calculate or assess the
value of the other person to one's plan of life. There is no attempt to make a judgment as to whether the marriage will be
rewarding in some practical way, such as producing bright
children or blending mutual interests. The B approach means

loving with one's total being, in response to feelings that cannot be rationalized. If called on to account for his love, the
person cannot defend it logically but can only answer, "because I love."

This kind of love can be disturbing. It is described in some
of the novels and movies that many people find upsetting,
wherein a person is consumed by love for another who is not
good for him, and both individuals are ruined. But whether it
is *Love Story* or *Romeo and Juliet*, this kind of love always
opens both persons to more of life than they would have seen
otherwise, and it evokes deeper and more profound feelings
than would otherwise be possible.

"Manhood" Versus Mankind

Now let us put together the pieces just described—the two
types of structure and the two kinds of perception.

The mechanical, logical, mathematical structure is to be
equated with the D approach because it means emphasizing
functions and values. It means solving problems for known
purposes. It means hurrying up a process, if possible, by
applying more resources, using schedules and programs, setting deadlines. Of especial importance, it means doing something because of its utility. One task is chosen instead of another because it will produce more reward and get the person
"farther along."

B-cognition, on the other hand, is to be equated with organic structure. It means seeing more than can be described in
terms of known function. You react, not to an "Italian," but to
a being who has qualities that may never have been described.
You choose a task because you like the "feel" of it, the feelings it evokes in you. You choose a mate because of what your
intuition tells you. You are content to let things grow and de-

velop in their own time, without manipulation or "crash programs" to hurry them up.

Can the two approaches be characterized as "masculine" and "feminine"? I believe so, at least, if we recognize that no person employs one quality or the other exclusively, but only emphasizes one or the other in his outlook. The feminine mind leaps to the whole, finds the answer without any steps in between. It is more reverent; it picks up things not in order to use them but to look at them and appreciate them. It is discursive; it wastes time. The masculine mind, on the other hand, concentrates on getting what it wants, shutting out interferences (including, sometimes, family and community), proceeding logically step by step, seeking to achieve and succeed in a preordained manner. It is efficient; it does not waste time if it can help it. It is exploitative—and it must continually prove and reassert itself. For instance, after the announcement that U.S. fighting forces had invaded Cambodia in 1970, a White House aide, talking to reporters, explained that the President had to show the world that "America hasn't lost its manhood." [22]

I suggest that our society stands in great danger from the masculine, mechanical, logical, D-cognitive approach to life. Efficient and valuable as this way has been, its effectiveness is declining. It has accomplished important objectives for mankind. It has produced a high standard of living and enormous gross national products for Western nations. But it has led to deficiencies in the form of disrespect for life's relationships, to impiety toward the delicate balances that exist between individuals and in the environment, and to ruthless disregard of people and things that appear (to the very practical, utilitarian mind) to stand in the way of achievement.

This is why the shadow of futility, as Bronowski called it (see Chapter 2), follows us through our affluence and successes. There is not one of us—I include the extreme cases of D-cognition such as Stalin and Hitler—who does not possess some elements of B-cognition or femininity. While we may achieve the most fantastic heights, set ever higher plateaus of need, and succeed in possessing them, our intuitive side is not satisfied. Instinct tells us that what logic and efficiency have attained is not enough. Exploitation, no matter how successful, is *never* enough.

Destruction by D-cognition

Let us look at some illustrations of the masculine, exploitative, D approach.

1. *War.* Perhaps there is no more vivid an illustration than war. Here the devices of the logical mind—its weighing of objectives and evaluation of methods in a rational, scientific way—are at their destructive worst. We decide that we shall prove a point or protect an ideal by destroying another people. After hostilities begin, we broadcast body counts of the dead in the media. When we want to take a certain hill or position, we decide whether it is worth the cost on the basis of an estimated attrition rate. Perhaps it is such a valuable hill that we would be willing to lose up to five hundred men in taking it. The whole military program is worked out with facts and computers, and every bit of it, every life lost, can be defended in logical, factual terms.

Obviously there is no room for femininity or B-cognition in this approach. What Jan Smuts once called "holism" must be shut out. We have to close our eyes to the subtle, mysterious relationships of the destroyed population to neighboring populations, and of those to their neighbors, and so on until the chain finally comes back to our own existence on the planet. How can complex relationships like those be priced?

2. *Industrialization.* Another illustration is industrial and commercial progress. During its periods of greatest growth, the maws of industry and commerce consumed all kinds of people. Families were uprooted in the name of efficiency; they were housed for the sake of better control; children were used because of the cost advantages; working conditions produced debilitating diseases, but the expense of treating the diseased worker and terminating his services was less than the expense of improving the air he breathed.

Although we do not go to these extremes today, it is seldom that anyone questions the validity of economic goals and motivations so long as they can be achieved within the constraints of modern safety and health standards. For instance, our highly competitive work system exacts a high toll in terms of the psychological well-being of many employees. Perhaps this is necessary—I don't know. But it is significant that practically no one protests the cost so long as competitiveness at work stimulates efficiency and output.

3. *Transportation.* When traffic becomes slowed down in a city, we examine the flow of movement and examine where the businesses are. Then we build roads through or widen the present arteries so that the flow will be accelerated and economic development stimulated (so much more sales volume, so many more jobs, and so on). If forty or fifty houses are in the way of the most logical construction route, we run bulldozers in. This costs so many thousands of dollars and will upset so many dozens of families in the community, we agree, but the economic value of bulldozing greatly exceeds the expense.

When it comes to airport expansion or facilities for the supersonic transport, we reason in much the same way.

I do not mean to diminish the necessity of good roads and airports. I use them, appreciate them, and would be seriously inconvenienced without them. But I think it is significant that only a few voices ever seem to ask, "Are other values being destroyed by this achievement in speed?" If we knew the answer, we might still go ahead as planned, or make only minor revisions, but we would not be denying that part of our nature which cries for the exercise of intuition, imagination, impression, sensing, and feeling for the whole reality involved.

4. *City planning.* We are used to thinking of our cities mechanistically and in terms of their utilities to commerce, government, communication, education, and other tangible needs. But as Jane Jacobs has pointed out in a fine study,[23] there is more to a city than mechanical structure. You cannot simply survey it, put the data through a computer, and find that there should be, say, a city park in every five square miles and shopping sections of a certain size every mile and a half. A city has an organic nature and can be appreciated only if the "tone" of its life is taken into account—its moods, its psychological qualities, its many dynamic relationships. The park is destructive or creative depending not just on how many people have access to it but on its environment; the shopping centers serve a variety of purposes that are not commercial; and so on.

The grandest economic goals for cities such as Detroit and Chicago fall short of the need for a satisfying community *life* in those places. No matter how much we achieve for such cities in quantitative terms—average living standard, volume of sales and production, clean air and water, and other measures —we will be haunted by the demand for "More, more!"

5. *Ecology.* We have assumed that mineral life exists to be used profitably, so we have mined it, paying little attention to the prospect that vast areas of nature would be spoiled in the process. Seeing animals in the world, we assume that they are there to serve our needs and pleasures—food, clothing, trans-

portation, sports. Rivers and lakes? For transportation, water supply, dispersal of refuse, recreation. Trees? For lumber.

In short, the natural world is seen in terms of functional values—what it can do *for us,* especially our physical, material needs. And we are suddenly waking up to the fact that to approach the environment in such a purposeful, utilitarian, D-cognitive way is to destroy it. We are dependent upon it; we cannot exploit it, drain it, and discard it when it is no longer useful, as if it were a tool or an appliance.

6. *Marriage.* As a final example, consider relationships in marriage. I do not know how many times I have listened to men complain: "What does she want? I gave her this, I gave her that, I did this for her and that. She likes these things. She has more of them than any of her friends do. What more could I do? But it isn't enough for her. What does she want?"

The answer, of course, is that she wants more than things, more than utilities. But the masculine mind cannot understand this. It would probably require a computer to add up the number of marriages that have soured because the male partners (sometimes the female partners) would not or could not approach the relationship in any other way. And the tragic aspect is that they never could see why they failed.

If We Fail

To sum up, we are not likely to fail, as individuals or as society, for lack of efficiency in manufacturing, distribution, organization, and/or technology. While all such activities will continue to be essential, our know-how in pursuing them is being well maintained. If our world of affluence and burgeoning opportunity blows up or caves in, it will be for causes unrelated to technical capacity and proficiency. If we find life in the West barren and disappointing, it will not really be for the lack of money, power, status, or luck—although that may be the rationalization—except in the most unusual cases. (I am quite aware how many Westerners live at economically sub-subsistence levels, with physical disabilities, and so on.)

In short, the fault will not be our achievements but our expectations, not brainpower or material power but understanding power and appreciation power. Strong men and women are trying to overpower their environment with their physical presence, fists, money, brains. No matter how many people they outmaneuver, beat up, or overcome, there is always someone or some group that remains to be defeated. The world does not respond to them. If we watch them closely, we will see the horror that comes to them as they realize that the people they have defeated have not been beaten and that there is still more to conquer. All their strength and achievement become as dirt in their mouths. "It didn't work. I'll have to try harder, do better the next time." They are like the legendary Sisyphus trying to roll his rock over the hill. Every time he gets it to the top, it rolls back and he has to start over again.

I am not belittling economic, social, or political success. It is wonderful to enjoy, and there is much fun and challenge in seeking it. I am saying only that it does not satisfy. This statement may seem naïve and incredible to many people; they are sure such success *will* satisfy when they achieve it. But, to paraphrase a famous ad, ask the man who owns it.

Women's Lib
and the Feminine Principle

Having examined some problems associated with masculine attitudes, let us turn now to the role of feminine values in U.S. society. To me, this is a question of enormous significance. I can think of no other question that has more far-reaching implications. I suspect, however, that perhaps the majority of Americans fail to appreciate these implications.

Let us begin with the women's liberation movement, since it is so well publicized.

The spiritual person is likely to be unimpressed by the women's liberation movement, not because it tries to go too far or too fast, but because it does not go far enough. From a spiritual standpoint, it is difficult to fault the basic principles the movement stands for. In fact, they seem elementary—even trivial in some respects.

I do not minimize the hard struggle in the past, or that which still remains, to accomplish the goals of women's lib. I am aware of how much resistance it has to contend with. I am aware that practically all of us men have biases built into our thinking by our traditional American culture (the conventional use of the pronoun "he" when referring to a person either male or female, is an illustration). But here is a movement that today involves such articulate and energetic Americans as Betty Friedan, Bella Abzug, Gloria Steinem, Dr.

Benjamin Spock, Senator Eugene McCarthy, and a great many others. Posthumously, one of the great intellects of modern times, Sigmund Freud, has been brought into the controversy again and again by prominent speakers and writers. Yet there is a shallowness about women's lib as its leaders conceive of it. It seems to have practically nothing to say about the real genius of women. For the lack of that genius, I am convinced, our society and the world at large are in danger of perishing.

The spirit can find no real argument with the proposition that women should have equality with men in every imaginable regard in the United States. They should have legal equality. They should be equal in the marts of industry; they should be able to do any kind of work for which they qualify physically and emotionally and which they want to do; they should receive equal pay for equal work performed. They ought to be able to live the way they want to live, to determine for themselves their mode of dress and their style of life. They should be able to determine for themselves whether they want to marry, to bear children, to be the heads or co-heads of their families. (In the next chapter I have more to say about the tragedy of casting women as sex symbols or as junior marriage partners who subordinate themselves to their husbands.)

Can anyone with spiritual values dispute any of these goals? Naturally there are legitimate differences of opinion over the desirable methods to employ in changing the "male chauvinist" policies of business, governmental, and other organizations. And of course there are honest differences over the question of how fast to go, and with what order of priorities. But while such questions of procedure and tactics are important to the short-term success of the movement, they are hardly basic. I have little doubt that the goals will be realized in this country—and swiftly. For this we can thank the movement's energetic leaders.

What is disturbing, from a spiritual standpoint, is that in all the speechmaking, writing, and demonstrations we are paying little attention to the accelerating loss of "feminine" qualities in our society. Now, by "feminine" I do not refer to genital or other physiological structures. A woman is not feminine, in the sense of the term as it is used here, because of her structure any more than a man is "masculine" because of his physiological structure. The point seems too ridiculous to mention, yet physiological differences lead us repeatedly to confuse the issue. Feminine qualities, as I write of them here, are not confined to women, not confined to mothers, not confined to pretty or subservient people. These qualities *may* express themselves in motherhood, but they may also express themselves in countless other ways. No one person could possibly embody all of them.

Feminine qualities are aspects of the spirit. Why we associate them with women is a question we need not go into here, except to note that the explanation may lie in the kinds of work women have done, the kinds of relationships they have had with men and children (however inferior those relationships may have been considered), the kinds of responsibilities they have had in the family and the community, and/or the kinds of clothes they have traditionally worn and the food they have eaten. If it is true that femininity is due to such factors, the currently changing life-styles of women could be more important than we realize. Will the feminine qualities be lost as women change in their social relationships and assume different responsibilities in the community? I do not know, but it is an important question for women's lib leaders and all Americans to be thinking about, and it should be studied carefully. Although I shall not try to answer the question in this chapter, I shall come back to its implications later.

WOMEN'S LIB AND THE FEMININE PRINCIPLE

The Feminine Approach

To begin, what are the feminine qualities of behavior? Eight stand out in my mind.

1. *Passivity.* So many women's lib leaders are opposed to passivity—and rightly so, given their aims and ideals. Obviously American women have been overly passive in their acceptance of conditions that should not be tolerated.

But there is another, more important sense of passivity. I refer to the attitudes of acceptance, appreciation of the world as it is, and lack of motivation to imprint one's self on the world or to "bulldoze" it into a desired form. Passivity in this sense is one of the most important characteristics of femininity. Although the world may be changed when people with this quality move through it, it is left essentially in its original form.

The feminine woman is willing to wait, for in her scheme of values nature has predominance over the ambitions of the human mind. Her patience sometimes drives men mad, for their desire, as we saw in Chapter 10, is characteristically to impose efficiency, production, control, and rationalization.

I must emphasize again that neither passivity nor the qualities to be described next belong exclusively to women. Men possess them too—sometimes to a greater degree than women. The qualities are classified as feminine because they are more dominant and characteristic of women than of men.

2. *Sense of wholeness.* The feminine person is more conscious and responsive to the whole of life than to its parts. She knows, from the earliest days of her being, that somehow or other a family, community, or society is greater than the tangible things and activities that can be identified in its operation. She does not see individual fulfillment in a specialized way. It

is more than getting ahead, or becoming rich, or living in Grosse Pointe. A living body is more than its chemical constituents. The economy is more than its gross national product. A war is more than a contest for territory, casualties, equipment, and power. And love, as Elizabeth Browning reminds us in her beautiful sonnet, cannot be broken down into constituent parts:

> If thou must love me, let it be for nought
> Except for love's sake only. Do not say,
> "I love her for her smile—her look—her way
> Of speaking gently,—for a trick of thought
> That falls in well with mine."

Being concerned with the whole, she is not so intent on managing efficiently, because the whole can *not* be manipulated, as only the parts can. Also, she is more concerned with feelings than with reason. She uses intuition. Her thinking is not characterized by conclusions arrived at through logical sequences of thought, but by understandings that come from deep within her and that are shaped by her acceptance of nature as she experiences it with conscious and subconscious perception.

This quality, too, may drive the masculine male to distraction. It accounts for some of the torment of husband-wife and male-female relationships in general down through the years. The masculine mind simply cannot comprehend the emphasis on feeling and tone over logic and reasoning.

I do not suggest that the feminine woman is unaware of or unappreciative of the male's specialization. She understands full well his skills, devotion, labor, and achievements—and she honors them. They are utterly necessary to her existence. If she is amused by the male's preoccupations, it is not because she rejects them but because she sees them in perspective.

3. *Sense of relatedness.* A closely connected aspect of femininity is the knowledge that things have meaning only

through their relatedness to one another. This is why woman has been called the guardian of the spirit, for the spirit, as we have seen, is an appreciation of relatedness. Woman has lighted the candles when there was need for something more than merely light or warmth. The candles symbolized spirituality for her, especially festivity, beauty, love. She has spent much of her time and some of the gains wrought by the male in doing things that were inefficient, inexpedient, seemingly unnecessary—yet eternally valid and true in the sense of being fulfilling. Better than the male has, she has understood the old truth that it profits a person nothing to gain the world but lose his soul.

4. *Dependence.* Understanding the relatedness of things, the feminine woman has been aware of her dependence on others. She has understood she could not "make it on her own" (and that neither can the male, though he may have thought he could). So she has been submissive, not in the sense of being helpless and frail but of understanding that she could not act without reference to the lives and processes that supported her life.

The masculine person traditionally has been unwilling to admit his dependency. He has considered so doing a sign of weakness. What the feminine person has realized instinctively is that dependency is in the nature of life and creativity. I believe that in a great many cases women have condescended to the male because of their superior understanding; they have played up to his masculine arrogance and failed to help him understand the weakness of his arrogance.

5. *Amateurism.* The feminine person does not make the commitment to doing and achieving that the person with a masculine temperament does. She may even be amused (at least, when she is not driven to tragic distraction) by his preoccupation with excellence in the activities he undertakes.

For example, if he is given to philosophy, he will indulge in it not for the sake of understanding. He will turn to philosophy, as he turns to cooking or golf, with professional zeal. No matter how ridiculous the notions that he strings together may be (at least, when judged by a person who is not so involved), they are of the utmost importance and significance to him, and he will become completely immersed and buried in them. In fact, if he is an exemplar of professionalism, he will take his pride, dignity, and sense of worth from his involvement in his chosen field of activity. Whether his skill is salesmanship, management, engineering, carpentry, accounting, or some other kind of labor, he will, if he is a strong man, lose himself in his work.

It is this approach which amuses the truly feminine woman. No matter how much she admires it, depends upon it, and profits from it, she wonders how any creature could so bury himself in a trade or profession! During a radio interview, the noted bridge expert Steinwald once observed that there were probably more "very good" female bridge players than "very good" male players, but that there were practically no females in the circle of topnotch tournament players. The reason, he felt, was that while women had just as much talent as men, they could not take bridge seriously enough to be in the very top circle. Only men could devote themselves single-mindedly to the game, as if nothing else mattered.

6. *Reverence for growth.* It is characteristically feminine to be concerned more about peace than war, more about love than competition. The woman is fascinated by the growth and development of her children. She is concerned with putting in their way whatever they need in order to grow, just as she does with a plant on the windowsill. She sees creativity not as a process to be analyzed and manipulated, but as a process to be understood. (She does not, for instance, try to dissect crea-

tivity and apply parts of it to more efficient production, as groups of men have organized to do.)

So she nurtures, heals, protects. She shields vulnerable individuals and groups from those who would change, engineer, and control society to serve a rational objective. The male is in a dilemma. While exasperated by the female's approach, he must yet turn to her for this quality of protectiveness and compassion.

7. *Capacity for play.* One of the most important feminine qualities, in my opinion, is an understanding of what play is all about. Unlike the masculine person, the feminine person knows that to take play seriously is to defeat the whole purpose of it. For example, she does not dive into it, as men so often do, as if her existence depended on it. Eda J. LeShan, author of several books on childhood, relates the following anecdote:

> Studying for his doctor's degree in psychology some years ago, my husband decided that he needed relaxation, and tried to teach himself to play the recorder. He struggled grimly for several evenings with scales and "Three Blind Mice," then he gave up. "Too much like work," he said, and went back to his books. Our four-year-old daughter discovered the instrument one morning on his study bookshelf. Holding it up expectantly, she put it to her lips and blew a high, quavering toot. Delighted, she skipped out into the sunshine, improvising a melody as she went along. My husband said to me later, "The moment she made that ridiculous sound, I knew she was playing the recorder as I had longed to—just playing it and having fun!" [24]

The male will do the same thing with sex. He will immerse himself in it with an unbelievable drive and intensity, priding himself on his prowess and capacity. While the female greatly values her role in sex, she finds his preoccupation amusing.

She reacts in the same way when, on occasion, he turns to his family and "makes a project" of togetherness.

Why does she react in this manner? Because she has the capacity to think of ideas experimentally, playfully. It is an approach we all can profit from. To illustrate from personal experience, in consultations with people I find the concept of "play" quite valuable. When I give someone an idea relevant to marriage, work, or self-fulfillment, I may say, "Play with it." I don't mean to be casual and humorous. I say, "Play with it," because I want him to throw the thought up into the air and look at it, see it turning around and upside down and inside out and falling into strange shapes. Then I want the person to pick it up and toss it once more, to see how the sun shines off it, to find out how it looks in the moonlight, to learn if he can see it when it is dark and he closes his eyes. I want him to act like a child playing with a ball or a kitten with a piece of cloth, to forget the utilitarian aspects of the idea and whether it will prove him stronger and smarter than somebody else. For it is the function of the spirit to play, celebrate, enjoy, and understand.

Some of the great Japanese men of wisdom have spoken this way, and in certain classes and groups it once became a way of speaking. A person would say something like, "I see that you are playing at arriving in Tokyo," or "I hear that your father has played dying." Is such an association of ideas shocking? Not in the view of the spirit, for it can play with death, not treating it casually but looking at its different forms and shapes, finding it always different. Instinctively the feminine woman finds it easier to do this than the masculine person does.

Contemporary theologians have paid considerable attention to the role of play in religious attitudes. Illustrative books are Harvey Cox's *A Feast of Fools*, Hugo Kahner's *Man at Play*, Wolfgang Zucker's *The Clown as the Lord of Disorder*, and

Sam Keen's *Apology for Wonder*.[25] And as Marcia Cavell points out, it may take years of effort for a person to reach the point where he can play, in the religious sense. Miss Cavell quotes Robert Neale on this point:

> Full play by the mature adult can be understood as the end goal of human development. Obviously, such experience is quite rare [and when it does occur] it is called "holy." Like Moses before the burning bush, the mature player takes off his shoes and kneels on holy ground. And like David before the Ark of God, he also kicks up his heels with delight.[26]

8. *Romantic attitude*. As is known by every sensitive man married to a feminine woman, she will often be dissatisfied just when he thinks she has everything. What husband is there who has not looked at his wife and thought (or said, in effect): "You have this and this, and they are what you said you wanted, aren't they? What more do you want?" Most males never get to understand that it is not the gift, act, place or achievement itself which satisfies the sense of feeling-awareness, but these things in relationship to the rest of life. In their frustration men may call the woman's attitude romantic and unrealistic. Romantic it may be, but not, in my opinion, unrealistic. It would be unrealistic, I agree, if the woman did not understand that we live in a world where we need food, clothing, and achievement; where we need capacity and strength for defense against our enemies; where there is a necessity of competition. But I know of few women who are unrealistic in that sense.

Contradictions and Counterplay

How do these feminine qualities rate in our society? There is a curious contradiction in our attitudes that we should be aware of, for it tells us something about both the problems we cope with and the kinds of solutions that will work.

Generally speaking, American society is masculine in attitude. As emphasized in earlier chapters, we are motivated to achieve, control, compete, organize. Masculinity characterizes even our religions, especially Judaism, Protestantism, and such other faiths as The Church of Jesus Christ of Latter-day Saints. Roman Catholicism has made a valiant attempt—in my opinion, a significant attempt—to introduce femininity into religion through the adoration of the Blessed Virgin Mary, and through other women in the hierarchy of saints. But for the most part our religions have been built around masculine deities.

The oldest one is Judaism's Yahweh. Many of his masculine qualities were inherited by Christianity's God. Although our concept of him today is generally less personal than it used to be, we still call upon him to support us in wars, athletic contests, space ventures. He defeats our enemies for us still; if people thought he did not, great multitudes of them would leave the churches. There are winners and losers, we say, and we do not have much time for losers. To be strong in competition, to be efficient, to manage successfully, to excel rationally —all these are considered moral and religious virtues.

But not all of the most important things in our lives are masculine. There are significant exceptions. Long before women's lib came on the scene, we were ascribing the feminine gender to highly valued institutions and symbols. Perhaps we never thought about it, in which case the habit is even more interesting and significant.

For example, we refer to our country as a feminine thing. However rough, competitive, warlike, and exploitative we have been, our country is *she*, and she is beautiful. Thus we attribute to her qualities above and beyond those material strengths which enabled us to make her great and worthy of our pride and awe.

Our flag is always *she*. "She's a grand old flag," we sing. Knowing that there is more to the United States than gross national product and armed strength, we make the Stars and Stripes symbolic of sacred, precious values. If someone desecrates or humiliates the flag, we cringe, not because commerce or the military have been harmed in any way but because our spiritual sanctity has been violated.

Our ships and trains are referred to as *she* because we think of them mysteriously and romantically, more than just carriers of people. When a man adores his automobile he calls it *she*. Women and other men may make fun of him, but usually the men, at least, understand: he is saying that there is something more than the physical features that endear the car to him.

A person's alma mater is always a lady. She is a nurturing, sponsoring, mothering agent in the student's life. When we sing the songs of our alma mater it is not with a sense of competition, even in the middle of a football game, but with a sense of adoration and devotion. It is in the cheers and cries that we vent the competitive, conquering urge.

Nature is "mother nature." We cannot begin to encompass her, even in all our textbooks, so we ascribe the feminine gender to her. She is too full of mystery and miracle to encompass with a masculine "he." The unconscious is also *she,* for it represents the dark, unknowable, awesome side of personality. (This is one reason that I prefer the term "feminine" to "female" in this discussion. The latter not only has a physiological connotation but suggests that, because of her female structure, any woman has the qualities and no man does. Both inferences are utterly wrong because the unconscious belongs to both sexes.)

How can it be explained that in our ostensibly masculine society we refer to some of our most sacred institutions, symbols, and objects as feminine? The contradiction reflects a deep and basic aspect of human personality: the masculine is always behind the feminine, and the feminine behind the masculine. They are a part of each other much as the black and the white are combined in the symbol of the Yin and Yang. When the feminine qualities shine forth in a person, masculinity lies behind them. Without it they would be perverse and ugly. Think of any of the qualities earlier described—for instance, passivity or dependence. If they were completely dominant, they would be objectionable in a person or a society.

The same thing goes for the masculine qualities. No matter how forcefully expressed in a man's personality, they have a feminine background or counterpart. Without that background, they would be grotesque. It is not coincidental that the great warriors in U.S. history have also been men of mercy after the conquest.

The great psychiatrist Carl Jung referred to the unconscious, dark background of the female personality as the animus. For the male, that unconscious becomes feminine, the anima. This is a way of indicating the mutuality, the utter necessity of the relationship. In the personality of an individual —or, it would be fair to say, of a society—there needs to be a balance of masculine and feminine qualities.

Now, the right balance is rare and difficult to achieve. It is hardly ever an equal balance, and in any case it depends upon a variety of circumstances. In many of us, the background— the hidden unconscious—comes too much to the fore. For instance, in the case of a woman, that which should be feminine may become weighted with masculinity; in the case of a man, masculine attitudes may become overly colored with feminine traits. In both cases a loss of quality and vitality results because there is not enough dynamic interplay between foreground (i.e., feminine qualities for a woman, masculine for a man) and background (i.e., the opposite).

Up until recent generations, nature depended on this conflict, I believe, to produce the human species. The conflict took place freely and naturally without much interference by the rational mind. But now that condition may be changing because of advances in psychiatry, chemistry, medicine, and other scientific disciplines. It could be that the interplay will be lost as a result of scientific efforts to control personality, and that humanity as we know it will be destroyed in the process. I do not predict this; I state merely that it seems to be a possibility in view of what scientists know today.

What does seem clear is that the United States grew vigorously and healthily as a young nation, not because it was solely masculine in approach, but because it possessed a dynamic balance of masculine and feminine qualities, a balance well suited to the needs of building a modern nation in a wilderness. The balance we need today is, of course, a somewhat different one. What I wish to stress now is the danger of losing a creative balance altogether. As a society we are moving in the direction of that danger, and women's lib seems oblivious to what is happening.

Let us look at the trend in more detail.

Risks in Downgrading Femininity

The qualities emphasized for modern women by women's lib seem to be masculine qualities—power, competitiveness, independence, control, exploitiveness. Now, the liberationists cannot be blamed for this approach; it appears to be an expression of our total cultural orientation in the United States. Also, it must be recognized that the economic, legal, and social equalities sought could not be won in a few decades without an aggressive campaign; an example of militancy on the part of the leaders has been a necessity. But I am not concerned here about the reasons. My concern is that the movement is washing out femininity among those women it influences.

As a result, women are led to become less concerned with tenderness and nurturing growth. Their efficiency and busyness is making them glossy, hard, shallow, and nonspiritual. They may not mind being described as "spiritual" if the adjective is used in a vague and sentimental way. But they do object if the term is used to connote such qualities as softness, openness, responsiveness, vulnerability, lack of specialization, or concern with the organic totality of things. The downgrading of women has been costly to our civilization in many ways, but the greatest cost may be the current rejection by women of their own genius as they struggle openly with men for equality.

Speaking at the Fountain Street Church a number of years ago, the great sociologist Margaret Mead said: "The most important quality for living today and in the future is punctuality and precision." That is correct insofar as the effort to compete successfully in a technocratic age is concerned. But are these to be the qualities we put *first* in all our living? Are we to leave no time for dreaming, for idleness, for gazing and musing and simply feeling?

It is my impression that home used to be an escape from organized efficiency. It is not now. Women have told me that the only time they find for meditation is when they are making the beds. In that homely activity, which has to be done and does not require thought, there is a moment of peace before they start engineering and organizing and running things! Getting the children to school, helping with the library or other special projects, busing students to band practice and football games.

After school there are dancing classes, music classes, special projects. During the evenings, Boy Scouts, Girl Scouts, Campfire Girls. During weekends, Little League, cleanup, science expeditions, shopping, parties. Carpools to get people around. Hurrying home to make dinner on occasions when the whole family happens to be there. Birthday parties, Halloween, Christmas shopping. There is no end to it. Many women tell me that when an evening or afternoon comes along when there is no need to organize and hurry, they don't know how to handle it. They fall asleep!

If there was a time when home offered some escape from frenzied activity, where children and husbands could rest and renew their spirits, it has gone with the wind. Women, too, are learning to prove their worth by the number of activities they do. Indeed, it may be that many women have to organize themselves even more than men do because of their fifteen-hour days and seven-day weeks! I am not saying that the projects are not stimulating and worthwhile. They usually are. And the involvement is valuable—it is through involvement and concern, we saw earlier (Chapter 9), that the spirit grows. What I am saying is that there is no room for femininity when activities and busyness become the *measure* of one's living. And where there is no femininity, there is no spirit.

The United States—and the world—stands in more desperate need of the feminine qualities than at any other time in its history. The conditions that once dictated emphasis on the masculine qualities no longer dominate. It took single-mindedness and drive to bring a wilderness under control. It took efficiency in exploitation of natural resources to build a modern civilization. But now many of those needs are being met or have been met, and there are quite different priorities —we are in a new ball game, as the saying goes. We need nonbusyness, nonactivism, nongraspingness, nonrationality, nonambition. We need gentleness, stillness, tenderness, forgiveness, meditation—the qualities that women find more natural to possess than men do, and that they are throwing away. In short, we need more emphasis on spiritual powers such as those described in Part II.

It could be that the feminine, irrational, subconscious qualities of feeling will one day erupt if we persist in subjugating them. When the religious leaders of the East referred (as have all spiritually-minded people) to the unconscious as dark, they were not being picturesque or trivial. They used darkness to symbolize a powerful force that could destroy the civilization built by the masculine mind. It may be that destruction is being hastened as women in the West, the East, and the Soviet Union join with males to wipe out the remnants of femininity. It is unlikely that we can violate an important part of our nature without paying a very great price. I make no predictions as to how, when, and whether such an eruption may happen, but I believe it is a possibility worth pondering. Its likelihood cannot be comprehended rationally, with decision trees and banks of computers. It is necessary to feel it and sense it, not to try to measure it.

Another possibility is that males will try to rescue femininity. Indeed, already we may be witnessing such a movement, albeit unconscious, in the concern of male youth for peace, nature, and love, along with their rejection of competitiveness, militarism, and industrial might. Other evidence of such a movement may be hippie dress styles, the rock, soul, and country-and-Western music young men prefer, the love-ins, and the experiments with drugs, communes, and encounter and sensitivity groups.

Unfortunately, males may not be well equipped for such a task. As pointed out earlier, feminine qualities are the male's background, and when he expresses them predominantly he lives in that background and is not effective. Likewise with the female: masculine qualities are her background, and when she emphasizes them she too lives in her background or shadow. Will either male or female be effective enough in such roles? Will the tension between them be deep enough to sustain viable human life on this planet? No one can answer such questions now, but they are worth mulling over.

One thing is clear: without more emphasis on the feminine qualities, civilization as we know it cannot continue much longer.

Love, Sex, and Marriage

Our American heritage and culture have many strengths, not the least of which is our willingness to examine our weaknesses critically and try to correct them. I can think of no weakness that affects more lives more profoundly than our attitudes toward love, sex, and marriage. To a dangerous and destructive extent these attitudes are vulgar, crass, muddied, opaque, and antispiritual. In the lives of far too many individuals and families, sex and love are freighted with so much superstition, ignorance, inhibition, frustration, and guilt as to take away the joy, vitality, and significance of sex, to degrade and destroy the institutions of marriage and family, and to rob love of much of its wonder, mystery, glory, and power.

This is a strong indictment, and it will be detailed from time to time later in this chapter. What I shall try to emphasize, however, is the positive side: how might a spiritual person think about love, sex, and marriage? To begin, six propositions will be proposed as a kind of platform for the spiritual approach to this important subject. These propositions are rooted in the qualities of the spirit explained in Part II.

Six Propositions for the Spiritual Approach

1. *Love is a relationship of interdependence between persons capable of appreciating, reverencing, and serving the ties of their dependence on one another.* This definition is not romantic-sounding, I know; neither is it theological in tone. I avoid both connotations purposely. What I stress is that love is both (*a*) the condition of interdependence and (*b*) the respect of and devotion to that condition. (If the reader wishes to apply theological language, he can call that condition of interdependence God, and the respect and devotion, love.)

As emphasized in earlier chapters, the spiritual person's concern is with loving relationships. These are what he seeks to understand, for they are the basis of his being and of the meaning of life to him. As just defined, love is the *sine qua non* of human life. Take it out of our lives and we would disappear from the face of the earth as surely as if thousands of hydrogen bombs were detonated in our midst. Of course, this cannot be said of romantic, altruistic, and other versions of love.

2. *Sex plays only a minor role in love.* Whether loving relationships are between two people, a person and a creature, a person and a thing, or a person and an abstraction (e.g., God, mankind, justice), the role of sexual desire is insignificant.

This proposition will sound naïve and absurd to a great many of us, I am afraid, because our movies, television dramas, novels, magazines, churches, and other cultural forces have dinned the opposite assumption into us. But that assumption does not hold up in everyday experience. To support this proposition I do not need to rely on my many years of counseling thousands of people on intimate problems. Let me simply speak now as a normal person reviewing average workaday behavior.

A great deal of sex *may* be involved in a person's love of an abstraction. For example, a nun who is completely devoted to her Lord Jesus Christ may describe her devotion to him in language that the psychologist recognizes as quite sexual. Again, a person's love for a piece of art, music, or ceremony *may* reflect sex; and there *may* be a perversion of sex in one's love of an animal. But these are extreme cases—not unusual in novels or abnormal psychology, perhaps, but rarely seen in our day-to-day lives. For most of us most of the time, sex does not enter into our love of animals, objects, principles and other abstractions, or one another. I am not rejecting psychological theory in this statement. Even the Freudians see the sex drive as buried deep in the base of human motivation, comingled with a number of other drives and urges.

Where sex *is* concerned with love, the cases generally involve an adult's relationship to someone of the opposite sex during a limited period of his and her lives. Sex is not significant in the love of children for one another, or of old people. And there is practically no sex involved in the ordinary adult's relationships with children, parents, aunts and uncles, brothers and sisters, friends, and associates.

In fact, there is less sex involved in the relationships of young people at the height of their sexual powers than our culture assumes. Parents raised in an earlier age are inclined to exaggerate the significance of extramarital sex today in communes, college dormitories, and other quarters. It is obvious that young people are far more permissive and uninhibited about sex than we, their parents, ever were. This means that those of them who have strong sexual urges are able to indulge those urges with relative ease. But I find, when I look into it carefully, that the attachments of many other young men and women are practically devoid of sex. Their relationships with one another are important—sometimes more important than those of couples sleeping together—and the omission of sexual activity cannot be attributed to physical, moral, or cultural barriers.

3. *Love plays a very minor part in sex*. We Americans used to relate the two. We made it a fetish to refuse to sanction sex without love. This custom of thought is still strong despite increased permissiveness toward 'sex. As a result, I believe that we have denigrated—and, indeed, to a large extent destroyed —both sex and love. We have put upon sex a burden that it need not and should not carry, just as we have put upon love a burden that reduces its wonder, glory, and power.

I do not assert that sex may not produce love. Nor do I assert that love may not produce sex. Both events happen repeatedly. But I ask: If you go back over your life, how many times was sex tied to love (as defined in my first proposition)? How much more often was sex the result of sheer physical pressure, desire, or excitement? Or precipitated by a sense of adventure, a desire to succeed in conquest, or social ambitions? Or generated by a sense of duty to another person? These latter relationships are the prevailing ones, in my observation and as I interpret the clinical data.

It is shocking that we have so little open discussion of this matter. To raise the subject in most groups of adults is to produce embarrassment, shame, and confusion—even in the relatively open climate of the 1970's. Is it not late for adults to act in so obscure and confused a manner about such a fundamental, human, organic thing as sex! We must understand and appreciate sex, not alone for the sake of sexual relationships but also for the sake of love. It is ridiculous to read sex into behavior as commonly as we do. Sometimes it seems that two men cannot be good friends without someone assuming that there is homosexuality in their relationship. Two women seen together often or sharing a home may excite the same comment. A grown person cannot cuddle a child without the parents becoming alarmed that his affection is sexually motivated.

I observe such reactions with horror. Until we appreciate sex as the natural, obvious, delightful human experience that it can be, and discuss it candidly, how can we free love from the intolerable burden of having to be expressed sexually?

4. *Sex plays a very limited role in marriage.* For reasons indicated, we have equated the two—again, to the shame and degradation of both. We consider man's most fundamental institution, that upon which society is based and many of our ideals rest, to be founded upon sexual relationships! We may no longer force a man and woman to marry when they become sexually involved, as we used to, but we say they "ought" to marry, and often we put pressure on them to do so. Once they are married, "anything goes" in the way of sex.

What does this do to the dignity of marriage? Is the sexual relationship really sufficient to give substance and meaning to our most important social institution? It is no wonder that marriages are being destroyed almost as quickly as they are made. If we equate sex with marriage, what happens when husband and wife discover that sex is not the all-powerful solution they once thought it was? What happens when they begin to experience the emptiness and boredom of sex, or when, as novelist Peter DeVries once noted, they have tried all the variations and run out of novelty? The answer is in our divorce courts.

There are happy, creative marriages where sexual relationships are strong and frequent. There are equally fine marriages where sex is infrequent or practically nonexistent. Clinical evidence abounds on this score. Yet we look at marriage as the legitimation of the sexual function. And at the same time we attach such "terrifying emotional significance" to sex, states Elizabeth Janeway, a fine observer of the Ameri-

can scene, that it becomes for many couples an extra source
not of pleasure but of concern:

> We are reaching the stage where any kind of enjoy-
> ment, but particularly the orgastic pleasure of sex, is being
> presented both as a duty to one's normality and as an
> achievement, but not as a natural, casual happening.
> People worry about their ability to please their partners
> and, worse, they worry about their own capacity to enjoy
> sex. Are their feelings commensurate with those that are
> represented on the screen or described in fiction? Do they
> respond with the proper frisson to nudity on the stage—
> which would surely not be set before them unless it was
> supposed to give them quite a thrill? If not, whose fault is
> it? This is such a simpleminded reaction that, on the face
> of it, it's funny. But the more baroque the novelist's treat-
> ment of sex, the more wildly Rabelaisian the comedy, the
> more often do ordinary human beings find themselves
> wondering uneasily whether they are not missing some-
> thing that everyone else enjoys.[27]

People of the spirit see that sex in and of itself cannot long
be exciting in marriage. They understand that it possesses little mystery and wonder except as a by-product of a loving relationship.

5. *In the courts and churches, sex is overemphasized.* In a
number of states still, adultery is the only justifiable excuse for
the dissolution of marriage; and in most of the remaining
states, it is perhaps the staunchest reason for dissolution. What
value do we give marriage when we make a sexual relationship outside of marriage the number one reason for termina-
tion? And what value do we place thereby on love? If love is
God, as Paul and others have told us, then in the eyes of the
law, love and God rest first of all on sex. This is absurd.

The other side is equally destructive and dreadful. For hundreds of years we have refused to let demonic marriages be

dissolved in our courts *unless* extramarital sex could be proved. In effect we have said to the complaining partner, "Go on back to your spouse and live in the horror." We allow a husband to degrade, demean, and destroy his wife; we allow a father or mother to bring shame and dishonor to the children, who thus become prime future prospects for our penal and mental institutions—all this so long as the partner has not gone outside the home for sex. Why does the law say this? It reflects the distortions in the popular understanding of marriage.

The Christian churches (with some notable exceptions) have been major contributors to this distortion. Isn't it interesting that Protestantism and Catholicism, which supposedly are concerned with the spirit, emphasize the body so much? At death they extol, glorify, and cry over the body—the Sacraments emphasize that. In marriage, the great crime in the eyes of the Christian churches has always been adultery. Some will defend the churches by noting that they had to be concerned with the problem of children born out of wedlock, potentially a more severe problem in centuries past than it is today. But this is a limited apology. How much did the churches have to say about the devastations on children wrought by morbid parental relationships and husband-wife abuses?

6. *The only valid, viable, just, meaningful ground for marriage is love.* Love, as defined earlier, is not affection, concern, or devotion to another person. It is not giving meaning to the other person, or using him or her to discover the meaning in one's own life. It is, as described earlier, a particular kind of relationship. Yet when two people love each other, the other values just mentioned come. Love has to come first, and always it is most important. If we exalt the by-product values instead, we succeed only in perverting and destroying them—

and love along with them. (For this reason, women's lib is on firm ground, in my opinion, when it objects to tendencies to make "sex objects" of women.)

Do I take something away? Those who have idolized sex know that nothing is taken away by these statements, because already they are losing, or have lost, the wonders of sex in their concentration on it. Those who have exalted affection, approval, or self-discovery know that nothing is taken away, for those qualities too have been lost in the search for them. However, when marriage partners love—that is, when they revere the ties that bind them—then, lo and behold, the qualities mentioned take hold and grow. The spouse becomes a wondrous person, with all his or her inadequacies, stupidities, and failures. We do not know how this happens. Affection, tenderness, and self-fulfillment were not with us yesterday, but now they are. It is as if they grew in the night. Someday, perhaps, behavioral scientists will be able to explain the process behind the fact.

The spirit sees marriage as a condition created to foster love, for it puts the partners into intimacy with each other. They are forced to depend on each other and to deal with the problems of growth. Made vulnerable by their interdependency, the partners become more sensitive to each other. When one tries to back away from this condition, there is a good chance that he will be stopped because of the other person who is involved. They can slip out, as often they do, but not as easily as they might in the absence of a marital commitment. If there are children, the significance and depth of the ties are increased.

A valid reason, in my estimation, for making divorce difficult is the importance of not letting a spouse run away easily from the pain of vulnerability. Many of us will try at least once to escape; and others of us will seek to turn away, or put up a shield to save us from the intrusions of intimacy and the potential threat to our selfhood. Yet these "dangers" are what make the relationship creative. Unless the risks are run, the benefits cannot be gained.

Marriage is a remarkable illustration of the interconnectedness of good and evil. The conditions that marital partners must live with until love can work its mysterious wonders are the same ones that may make marriage a sheer, unlivable hell for the partners. Vulnerability, intimacy, dependence upon each other—these are the ties that bind, and from them may grow satisfactions, joys, and creative possibilities that cannot be obtained in any other way. But the ties also produce hatred, resentment, jealousy, bitterness. I know of no marriages where this is not true.

Husband and wife do not want those unpleasant byproducts, and even less do they want the unpleasant sensations of intimate interdependence. So they will not go through the fire of the experience unless they feel devoted to the ties; instead, they will build walls between themselves, or retreat to a distance from each other (an emotional distance if not a physical one). A person does not hate someone who is at a safe distance—the casual friend, say, or the "ship passing in the night." In that kind of relationship the ties are slender and uncertain, just as the creative possibilities are.

Is it necessary to sacrifice one's individuality, pride, and independence in order to gain the more satisfying experiences of love? I think not—at least, not for long. For the fact is that the ties are there whether we like them or not; we *are* vulnerable, we *are* intimate with mankind, we *are* dependent upon one another, spiritually as well as biologically and economically. Marriage is not a creation of such ties but a recognition and confrontation of them. Moreover, the wonderful thing is that when a person gives himself in devotion *to the ties*, not to the other person, dependence becomes independence, vulnerability of self becomes strength of self, the involvement that is so dreaded becomes freedom.

Directions of Change

What do these realities mean for marriage in America? Are changes in our policies and attitudes needed? If so, what kinds of changes?

I do not see how an American can view marriage with thoughtfulness and feeling and fail to conclude that change is needed. No matter how data on divorce and broken homes are analyzed, the institution seems to be in a bad way. Rather than cite figures for the nation as a whole, let me try to bring the problem home by pointing to my own city of Grand Rapids.

Sometimes statistics on a problem are discounted because they reflect parts of the country that are unusually poor, turbulent, or unstable. No one can say that about data for Grand Rapids. It is a pious city—people sometimes refer to it as a "city of churches." I doubt that any other city in the United States possesses more churches per capita than this one does. In addition, it is a city of homeowners and people who are characteristically gentle, kindly, pious, and seriously attuned to their responsibilities. Grand Rapids also has a strong sense of tradition. Many Calvinist people live here; they work and play in their churches and communities and seek to bring their children up in the way of their ancestors. A large number of Roman Catholics live in the area too. Accordingly, one would surely expect that the institution of marriage would be treasured and revered here, and would appear in the best possible light.

What are the facts? Let me cite just a few of them:

1. In the past 27 years in Kent County (which includes Grand Rapids and its immediate environs), there were 80,712

marriages and 40,391 divorces—one divorce for every two marriages! [28]

2. The incidence of divorce is increasing.

3. There are 775 neglected children in the ward of the court. There are 525 delinquent children. Altogether, 1,300 children are legally classified as in trouble.

4. One out of every 4.25 families in Kent County is a broken family.

5. Our venereal disease rate is higher than the national average.

It seems clear that we need some new ideas about marriage if the situation is so bad in a fine, conservative, relatively stable, religious area such as Kent County! What changes should be sought? Keeping the spiritual orientation developed earlier, I suggest four desirable goals.

First, we should seek to make sex, sexual relationships, and sexuality joyous, loving, and natural for people of all ages—children, adolescents, young adults, and older adults. Sex should not be seen as mean, dirty, or unworthy. It is something we should rejoice in as a wonderful, natural human condition. Many programs of sex education in American schools and churches are commendable; we need to advance in this way on a broader front.

Second, we should hasten the coming of the day when people will not marry for sex. Sexual relationships should not be used as a club or pressure for making two people marry. To emphasize an earlier point, it is hard to conceive of a poorer basis for marriage than the legitimization of sexual relationships. That tradition has produced guilt, inhibition, and frustration in countless homes; it has made many of us frightened in our approach to marriage.

As a concomitant rule, sex should be deemphasized in divorce proceedings. Marriage is debased by laws that place sole or major emphasis on extramarital sex and consummation of sexual relationships. The only thing that really counts is the attitudes of the marital partners. This does not mean that divorce should be "quick and easy." It simply means that the dissolution of marriage, like its formation, should be based on the importance of love.

Would the development of such an attitude cheapen sex— and possibly marriage too? I believe that just the opposite would happen: sex would gain more dignity and be treated more honestly, and marriage would become a nobler, worthier, more respected institution. Greater equality of the sexes could be achieved. One aspect of our vulgar overemphasis on sex is praise of pseudo virtues like virginity for women before marriage, followed by the expectation of submissiveness to the male's sex drive during marriage. With such a dual standard it is no wonder that love, predicated as it is on equal dignity of the partners, has failed so often.

Third, we should work toward the day when couples marry for the sake of having children or for companionship (or both). Children should not come as an accident and unexpected burden. Sex may be an expression of companionship but not the only one nor the most important one.

Indeed, it seems likely and desirable to me that not all couples should be allowed to have children. Only willing, responsible couples should enjoy this privilege. Spiritual Americans will think of children as belonging to the community, not just to their parents.

Sociologist Leo Davids, of York University, Toronto, Canada, predicts that our future society will require people to obtain licenses before becoming parents, because it will want to assure that each child is brought up in a good home atmosphere. As evidence that this trend is already forming, he notes that "young people are gradually rejecting the myth of 'parenthood is fun,' realizing that parenthood is a very serious business and one which ought to be undertaken only when people are ready to plunge in and do a good job." [29]

Fourth, we should set as a goal that there be no unwanted, neglected, or abused children in our society. Such a goal would have significant implications for the reduction of crime, emotional illness, suicide, divorce, and immorality. It is an attainable goal if sex is freed of guilt and if children are born only to parents who want them.

13

A New Moral Code

Moral codes are devised in order to make it possible for people to live in community. Such codes are a recognition of the fact that individuals and groups are inextricably interrelated. They are maintained because of the desire of people to live in interdependence without destroying one another in the heat of the everyday frictions and irritations of community life; they are a kind of public defense against man's motivation to exploit the treasures of human community and of the earth. Prohibitions against assault and battery, for instance, are curbs on the destructive tendencies of man; without them, people could not relate to one another creatively and joyfully.

Over and beyond the need to survive, morality represents society's attempt to raise itself above the lowest common denominator of behavior and develop ideals of community living that people can aspire to. The injunction to love thy neighbor is an example of such idealism.

The conditions and understanding on which morality is based are always changing. It is essential that the codes change to reflect the new circumstances. If appropriate revisions are not made, the codes lose their validity, their usefulness for individual self-fulfillment and community survival; morality is then abandoned and lost. This practical, pragmatic aspect of morality has been demonstrated repeatedly in history, yet we tend to lose sight of it. It is inconvenient and difficult to revise moral codes when they become out of phase with conditions and understanding, but it is utterly necessary to do that if morality and community are to be maintained.

One reason for the chronic anxiety and uneasiness of Americans today is the growing recognition that parts of our codes are no longer valid. We may resist acknowledging this fact in rational ways, because it threatens standards and institutions we have held dear since childhood, but we sense it and feel it. To make matters worse, it is by no means clear to most people what new conditions and understandings morality should take into account.

We seem to be living between two worlds: one dead though fondly remembered, and the other struggling to be born. We are caught in a no-man's-land, for we have not yet had enough time, experience, and insight to formulate rules of conduct for the world that is emerging. The old codes are becoming increasingly unenforceable yet we cannot impose new rules because the new ideas and circumstances to be reflected have not evolved clearly. While the evolution is going on every day, with both young and old working at the task of reformulation (though they may not be aware of it or think of it in these terms), sufficient evidence of the direction in which we are headed has not accumulated to make the writing of new codes possible.

I smile sometimes, when I do not get angry, at adults who blame young people for being confused about what is right and wrong. No one is more confused than we adults! We may sanctimoniously proclaim some traditional rules for behavior at work, in social gatherings, and in bed, but if we examine our lives with any kind of objectivity and discernment, we will see that we too are terribly confused. Those of us who worry about the behavior of young people might do better to worry about the practices of the adult population and the nation's leadership!

In what ways is American morality changing? In previous chapters we have examined changes in such areas as the family and women's rights. Let me draw attention to some others.

Obedience is a good case example. Millions of Americans still believe in the Pauline injunctions of obedience to God. But how do we come to understand what God wants? There is no convincing answer. Various individuals and groups may believe *they* understand God's will, but the claimants understand it in conflicting ways and none of them can make a satisfying case that he knows. And who or what is God? Here the confusion grows. Differences of opinion are becoming so rampant, even within religious sects and among the parishioners of individual churches, that it is obvious only that we as a people do not know. Whereas in the past the church arrogated to itself prior knowledge of the will of God, and people accepted that knowledge, it is clear in the modern world that the church's claims cannot be validated. (Ecclesiastical edicts concerning birth control and premarital sex relations are perhaps the most obvious examples.) Therefore obedience to God has become a meaningless moral injunction for Americans. We do not know how to live without the authority of the church in this respect, nor do we know what new codes, if any, should be formulated to cover the gap.

What about obedience to parents? Such obedience has been part of the moral code in most civilizations for centuries. But the life-and-death power that American parents once held over their children no longer exists, except possibly in the stages of infancy (and then parents no longer possess the *right* to let a baby die, mistreat it, or sell it). Accordingly, parents can no longer demand and get obedience from their children.

Obedient many children are—sometimes to an advanced age —but as a matter of choice, not morality.

What about the old religious injunction that servants should be obedient unto their masters? Countless wives have sworn to obey their husbands, but that pledge is a fiction except in a dwindling number of cases, as the raft of jokes about it imply. We do not think of wives as "servants" anymore. Much the same applies to domestic help, corporate employees, government employees, and military subordinates. Outside the totalitarian countries it is difficult to find people who can be called "rulers." Yet there needs to be a morality governing the relationships between decision makers and those who implement decisions.

As a second example of a broad area in which our morality has been changing, consider private property. For many centuries property has been sanctified. Upon acquiring the legal ownership of a piece of land, chattel, or sum of money, a person could do with it what he pleased; he was beholden to no one. But today the notion of private property is no longer clear. For instance, to whom does the waterfront around Lake Michigan belong? Can the steel company that paid dearly for part of that frontage use it in any way it wants for draining waste water? What about your backyard? Can you use any kind of incinerator you want there? At the national level, can the Pentagon conduct a bomb test on a U.S.-owned island in the Pacific without regard to whether it threatens the Japanese?

The venerable commandment "Thou shalt not steal" is still firmly entrenched in our moral codes. Yet it is aboveboard and legal, experts tell us, for a small minority to steal from the majority when annual taxes are due. Some taxpayers who make millions of dollars annually reportedly pay nothing or practically nothing to the Internal Revenue Service; in fact, a

Treasury Department study of tax-law loopholes shows that 112 Americans with incomes greater then $200,000, including three with incomes in excess of $1,000,000, paid no federal income tax in 1970.[30] Are these people stealing from us? They do not think so—and not in the eyes of the law. But if you and I carry some of the financial obligations they should and would be carrying, but for legal technicalities, we are victimized just as surely as if they took from our bank accounts.

What about stealing from insurance companies and other corporations? They are considered fair game today if you can steal legally. Seasoned observers report that it is common practice in many states for garages to inflate auto repair charges paid by insurance firms. In most large companies it is common knowledge that expense accounts are often padded. An endless variety of such examples could be given, but the point for all is the same: no moral degradation is attached to the practice, and no one is taken to court for stealing. Yet it is theft in the real sense of the word.

Levels of Moral Behavior

Discrepancies such as those described are significant because, as emphasized earlier, morality as a whole begins to fail when it no longer reflects current conditions and public notions about behavior. To put it more bluntly, the alternative to a new moral code for America is no morality at all. This holds true in such vital areas as sexual behavior, domestic relations, working relationships, personal privacy, and private property.

Before considering substantive changes, we need to consider the dynamics of morality. What kinds of forces and compulsions can be used to enforce a moral code? What kinds of guides are possible? Important options are available, and the choice of them can make a major difference in our approach. I like to classify morality in terms of five levels. (This classification corresponds in some respects with those being worked out by academicians studying the subject.) Examples of these levels are shown in the chart "Levels of Morality."

The *first level* is behavior dictated by the fear of punishment. This is the level most of us had implanted in our minds when we were young: we did what good children were supposed to do because our parents would hurt us if we did not. Needless to say, this common approach to morality is a primitive one. If we do what is good out of fear of punishment, our behavior is determined by other persons, and we can claim no moral credit or honor for our acts. Surely all Americans should pass beyond this level quickly in their lives. In any enlightened community today many parents can be found who do not believe in any kind of punishment for their children. They see such punishment as an expression of a grievance, not tutelage; at best it produces a decorum they like, but not the enhancement of children's spirit and character.

Of course, the punishment may come from persons other than parents. If a person is "good" because he fears that some authority or perhaps God will hurt him if he misbehaves, that is first-level morality. This level is in evidence in many parts of our society. Indeed, many people apparently consider it to be *the* basis of morality—but it does not satisfy the spiritual American. Its possibilities are far too limited.

The *second level* is behavior dictated by fear of displeasure among one's family, friends, or associates. I think of this level as spiritual blackmail because it is enforced by the threat that feelings will be hurt or displeasure incurred. No club is used, no bodily injury is incurred, but the power to alter valued relationships is brought to bear. For example, parents let it be known that if children do not act nicely, the parents will not be proud of them; a wife mopes and looks forlorn when her

LEVELS OF MORALITY

UTOPIAN:
Setting one's standard of neighborliness higher than custom or law requires because of convictions about human relatedness

REASON AND LAW:
Rules concerning parental obligations to children or representations in selling goods

SELF-INTEREST:
Acting in the community interest because in the long run "what's good for the town is good for us"

FEAR OF DISPLEASING OTHERS:
Voting against a legislative proposal in order to please a strong constituent interest

FEAR OF PUNISHMENT:
Conforming to a parent's desire in order to avoid getting spanked, disinherited, or rebuked in front of the family

husband returns late from a poker game; a minority group tells a legislator representing the district how unhappy it will be if he votes in such-and-such a way on a bill under discussion; or powerful interests in a church tell the minister about their displeasure with some of the ideas he supports.

Thus the individual is coerced into behaving in a desired way by people who have power over him. Such actions often lead to enormous injustice because, again, the individual loses the sense of responsibility for his actions. In fact, after being manipulated repeatedly in this manner, he may get in the habit of using the power group as an excuse for not taking responsibility on himself—an old story in political and business life.

Accordingly, this level of morality, while slightly better than the first, is also inadequate from a spiritual standpoint. The individual *can* follow his own convictions and refuse to be cajoled—some do—but in reality individualism is discouraged.

The *third level* might be called self-interest; in its best form, it can be called enlightened self-interest. We take personal responsibility for our actions because we know that no one else is qualified to do that; also, no one else is going to look after us in this life. Appreciating that we are dependent upon others, and they upon us, we nevertheless recognize that others count on our looking after ourselves. If we are forward-looking, we know that we cannot go on for long at the expense of the community; therefore we try to develop mutual interests so that our achievements will accrue to the community's benefit as well as to ours.

To many intelligent people, this is the ultimate level of morality. It has indeed been one of the ingredients of a good society, and with increasing frequency it has become a mark of modern professionalism in business, law, medicine, architecture, accounting, and other fields. For example, Donald S. MacNaughton, chairman and chief executive officer of The Prudential Insurance Company of America, played a leading part in the decision of many life and health insurance companies in 1971 to channel more funds into enterprises involved in public health and community improvement. "We have a responsibility to place our investment funds, and they are considerable, where they will inure to society's benefit," Mac-

Naughton said. "This is not inconsistent with maximum yield, because in determining yield, we must take into consideration the effect of our investments on society as a whole, and over the long, not the short haul." [31]

Clearly this understanding of morality is more desirable than the first two from a spiritual standpoint. Let us hope that this philosophy grows in use. Yet the incentives, pressures, and aspirations even at this level are not good enough for Americans. For the concern of the individual and of the group is self-centered: they do things for others and for the community in order to get rewarded. Much of the morality that goes on at this level might be called "the professional salesman approach." The salesman is nice to the customer not because he truly likes him or is glad to see him but because he hopes thereby to make a sale. Or, to use a broader analogy, we cast our bread upon the waters not out of a conviction that it is good to be generous but in the hope of getting a larger amount of bread back.

The *fourth level* of morality is reason and law. Recognizing that we are animals and that animals must be regulated and restricted, we establish rules, police forces, and punishment procedures. It is difficult to conceive of a happy, creative society on any other basis. This is the highest level of morality yet devised by society. We go to the other people and communities that differ from us, and we say: "We will set up laws to govern our behavior and help us relate to one another. You need them as much as we do." Every person is created equal in the eyes of the law. All people must learn to respect the standards and help others to observe them properly. When the rules are found inadequate, they are revised by democratic procedures.

Despite the intellectual and organizational support given this approach, it is still an ideal, even in the United States. In

one community after another, individuals of different colors,
creeds, and financial circumstances are not in fact on the same
basis before the law; and there is a long way to go in developing voluntary support of the rule of law—even massive police
forces and large staffs of inspectors are not able to compel sufficient public observance of legal and regulatory codes.

Even this fourth level falls somewhat short of the ideal,
however. For as Joseph Fletcher has pointed out,[32] it is not
possible in a complex society to write rules that are equitable
and just in all cases. For instance, the commandment "Thou
shalt not steal" is a good rule—probably as good a standard as
can be devised for society. But is it wrong to steal in *every*
conceivable set of circumstances? Not even from a source of
plenty in order to keep a child from starving? Or to obtain ur-
gent and essential medical supplies? Again, consider the laws
against homicide. Suppose that only the killing of an insane
platoon leader can save the lives of the other men in the platoon.

Now, there is a higher level of morality still. This *fifth level*
might be called utopian because it does not seem practicable
for society as a whole in the foreseeable future. But it is a
level that *some* individuals and groups can rise to. I have seen
proof of this in my own community, and I know that the same
could be said of certain groups in many other cities and
towns.

This highest of all levels is, I believe, the one that Jesus and
the disciples used to talk about. "The law is good, but it is not
good enough." They were talking about the religious laws of
the Jewish people, but the point is pertinent nonetheless. Paul
said (I paraphrase): "I know you cannot live outside the law
or without it, but you cannot live only in and through the law.
You must rise above it." And he added (I paraphrase again),
"When you find the basis of your salvation, you can neglect

and ignore the law because you transcend it." The individual can transcend it in that case because he has worked out higher standards for himself: he respects and recognizes the law, but it is his minimum standard, somewhat like a minimum wage law for an employer.

This fifth level is understandable to and within the reach only of spiritual people. It assumes that the individual is willing to acknowledge the selfish, predatory animal in him, but mature enough to embrace that body as a friend, not reject it and hide it as an enemy. It is the person who does *not* come to terms with the primitive, irrational, destructive forces within him who is a moral hazard, for he drives those forces underground where he cannot deal with them. Failure to recognize this has been one of the most serious blind spots in American society. Since the beginning of our history, large numbers of people have subscribed to the naïvely idealistic notion that if saintliness could somehow be exalted in a personality, the devil could be driven out. But the devil is our "brother." So this notion has never proved out. Often it has, in fact, produced just the opposite of the intended effect.

In short, we have to know who we are in order to control ourselves. Knowing that, we take a giant step not toward chains but toward liberation and creativity. We find it easier to accept our dependence upon others, and their dependence upon us. It becomes increasingly possible to respect the ties that bind us to the community-at-large.

What I call the fifth level of morality is not new in the world. Religionists and idealists of almost every generation have conceived the possibility of a utopian community. Many young people today are pursuing the same vision. Knowing our nature, we will try not to abuse other people or destroy any aspect of our environment. Treasuring our interrelatedness, we will avoid being offensive to others.

History does not yet contain examples of such utopias that have worked, but the ideal continues to be held high. It is possible that more than a few Americans will someday achieve it.

Some Principles and Guidelines

As we work to develop more relevant and creative moral codes for America, what principles will help us stay on the right track? I want to propose five, stating them in a negative form because this provides maximum generality (to be valid a moral principle must be general). As we use these guides to formulate specific codes in different areas, such as domestic relations, property, and corporate conduct, we will often want to state the rule in positive form. It will be seen that all these guides are based intimately on the nature of spirituality as described in Part II.

1. *Do not abuse or take advantage of another person.* This principle is much broader than the traditional "Thou shalt not steal," yet it involves some of the same elements and is equally pertinent to personal moral relationships. It means that we must not take advantage of any powers or leverage we possess in order to exploit another person or group.

For example, we must not use our masculinity, femininity, strength, authority, status, maturity, or youthfulness to manipulate another person. Nor is it permissible to do the opposite, that is, use our weaknesses or vulnerability as a means of cajolery (e.g., making a point of how hurt or lonely we will be if a loved one is away on a holiday). In the area of business, this principle means that we must not take advantage of privileged information to the hurt or detriment of others, as when corporate insiders use knowledge of an impending real estate transaction or mineral discovery to enrich themselves before other investors can share in the knowledge. It would also apply to leaders in government who, having privileged access to unpublicized plans and decisions of public officials, could take advantage of individuals and organizations that are not privy to the information, or could use the knowledge to enrich friends and associates.

This principle has been serving as a guide for many young people in the difficult area of sexual relations. If one does not exploit another's weakness, ignorance, immaturity, or physical or physiological need, then sexual relationships are not immoral for them. Naturally, the principle requires intelligence, sensitivity, and a high degree of personal responsibility in everyday application. Because it does not specify particular actions that are permissible or impermissible, it does not allow an individual to escape responsibility for his acts by mechanical adherence to the provisions of a code or law. As many people know, it is easy to be immoral while following the letter of the law!

2. *Do not diminish another person or group.* In a world that has become as small as ours through communications and transportation, we must find ways to guarantee integrity of self and to protect valid differences among people. We must do this, for example, in meeting opposing moral viewpoints, opposing economic and political systems, contrasting and diverse religions, varying social customs, and people of a different color. In all cases we must seek to grant a maximum of dignity and respect to the other person or group, no matter how much we may feel that the thinking of the other person or group is not suitable for our own groups or as a general principle for mankind.

To illustrate with just a few specifics, this principle means that we do not condemn a Communist group because its ideol-

ogy threatens capitalism; we do not act impolitely toward a
radical campus group that seeks to destroy college as we know
it; we do not turn our backs on a person indicted or convicted
of preaching revolution; we do not mock a small powerless religious sect trying to conform to quaint or bizarre notions of
behavior. Of course, the principle does not mean that we give
in to such groups; we must not allow them to diminish us,
either.

3. *Do not betray your humanity.* As American society has
become more complicated, pressures have grown to reduce relationships to a mechanical level and to substitute anonymity
for individualism and personality. Individuals and families set
priorities, at first in a frank and necessary attempt to help
them manage their time, but with a tendency, as time goes by,
to put priorities on friendships and associations on the basis of
what is financially, politically, or socially advantageous. In
subtle ways the concept of "cost effectiveness," originally used
in the military and in big business to rank courses of action according to their dollar costs and returns, spreads into the in-
terpersonal behavior of people, so that, acting in the way that
ambitious and self-seeking persons always have, only more
efficiently than ever before, they budget their personal contacts on the basis of practical utility.

With growing complexity and sophistication in the handling
of complexity, therefore, we must make an unusual effort to
preserve our sensitivity, responsiveness, interest, and concern
for others—because they are people, not because they can advance us in some way. It is tempting to justify increasing
selfishness and self-centeredness on the grounds that public
welfare, corporate programs of community responsibility, and
other organizations are meeting the economic, social, and cultural needs of people with increasing effectiveness. That kind

of reasoning does not hold up. It represents a quick and easy way to a faceless, spiritless society.

4. *Do not seek to possess.* This is the negative form of the venerable injunction to share our gifts and treasures. We must grow in awareness that the things that are ours in legal title are ours only temporarily. The raw materials of the land and the skills that design and manufacture the materials are, in effect, lent to us for a while. The land and its resources were here before we arrived, and the human skills are descended from generations that lived before we arrived. The process will continue after we die, with others being the recipients of such loans while they live.

I can see a time not too far in the future when the natural wealth of the world—land, minerals, energy, human talent— will be considered as belonging to all mankind and not alone to the people who happen to have the treasures within their national boundaries or within the tracts of land to which they have title. This is *not* a prediction that communism is the wave of the future, that capitalism has outlived its usefulness, that property rights should be abolished, or any other such "anti-American" doctrine that some may be tempted to charge me with. Rather, my point is that a person of the spirit will increasingly reject acquisitiveness as a life-style. He will respect and uphold rights to use and enjoy property because creative and happy communities are not possible without such rights; but he will interpret the undisputable facts of our relationship to the earth and other people to mean that he must use his possessions with a keen sense of trusteeship—as a steward, not a coveter or an exploiter.

Property rights are necessary to freedom. If I cannot leave my skis outside the lodge for fear they will be stolen, my freedom of action is restricted in an unnecessary and undesirable way. But possession of property takes on different significance once one moves beyond everyday necessity into personal values and philosophy. The sin of possession, as it is sometimes called—of owning in order to feel secure, to dominate, or to control other people—may well be the basic sin. Religions other than Christianity seem to suggest this. For instance, Buddha, going farther than the monks of his time, said that man must reach the point where he feels no desire at all and, having no desire, finds all of God becoming his because he does not seek to take anything from Him.

Possessions will not protect us. Jesus emphasized the point repeatedly. He told the young ruler to go away and sell all of his goods. He was saying to him: "Your things are in the way. If you don't hold on so tightly, maybe you'll find valuables that do not have to be held on to." Now, Jesus didn't mean, I am sure, that a person should not possess goods. "All these other things will be added to you," he said. It was perfectly clear to him that we cannot live without owning things. He was talking about a person's point of view, about the things from which one hopes to obtain the real satisfactions in his life. Using the language of today, he might have said: "You're clinging to your goods, man, and that's what's stopping you. Let go. Let go! Cast your bread on the waters, don't try to hold it. Don't try to save your life. Lose it! Give it away and it will come back to you."

I like to think about my land and house this way: The land was there a long time before I was, and I trust that the land and the house will be there long after I'm gone. They were lent to me, I enjoy them for a while, I lend them to someone else when I am through. I don't have to cling to them. I don't have to make them mine by a writ of deed, however much that may be legally necessary if I am to enjoy the house and land for a while. I can deed or will the land to my children, but it will be lent only for a while to them too.

5. *Do not neglect the environment and life of the future.* Americans today have an obligation to future generations not to spoil the environment for them. We should feel obliged to hand on the earth's treasures and resources undiminished—if possible, enhanced and enriched. It is immoral for us to use the water, air, earth, vegetable life, animal life, and other resources as if there might be no tomorrow.

During the oil blowouts off Santa Barbara in 1969, militant citizens sat down in front of oil trucks, picketed the chamber of commerce, and urged county and city officials to obey an "eleventh commandment." This commandment was called "an extension of ethics to include man's relationship to his environment: Thou shalt not abuse the earth." [33] As Nietzsche said a hundred years ago, there is a new sin in the world, "a sin against the earth." [34] All over America there is a late but rapidly dawning consciousness that such matters as DDT in the soil, mercury in the sea, the extinction of snow leopards, the murder of eagles, and the eradication of sea otters in some areas cannot be viewed with detachment because they are part of a complex life chain on which we are intimately dependent.

But the physical environment is only part of our moral commitment to the future. We are under a singular obligation to treasure the gift of human life, to revere, enhance, and pass it on joyfully to the future. It is immoral to endanger the future of man in any way, whether biologically, physiologically, educationally, militarily, or by other possible means. Needless radiation hazards, excessive pollution, execution, burning of books, destruction of art, cruelty toward children—acts such as these are immoral because they either eliminate future life or jeopardize the enjoyment and appreciation of it.

Part IV

SPIRITUAL
LEADERSHIP

14

A More Mature
American Dream

We began this book with an examination of the rise of a new type of individualism in America. People want to be their own heroes now; they want to "do their own things." They are not willing to let rulers or authorities determine their life-styles. Then we analyzed the frustrations that people encounter when they try to find self-actualization (as behavioral scientists call it) through affluence and achievement. We saw that the self-actualizer of today is going to find the deep satisfactions he yearns for only through a spiritual approach to life—not turning his back on the practical world but broadening his concerns so that the spiritual is combined with the practical and makes it meaningful. Next we examined some problems of identity and morality that concern Americans.

But of course no one, not even the most individualistic young person today, forms his values and dreams in a vacuum. His thoughts are influenced by the ideas and ideals of society. This brings us to the question of the nation's hopes and aspirations, and, in particular, of the dreams of a spiritual society.

J. J. Greene, Minister of Energy and Resources for the Dominion of Canada, made a speech in Denver in May, 1970, that must have struck a chord with many Americans in the audience. Endeavoring to explain the often-critical attitude of many Canadians toward the United States, he said:

Part of the cause for the rise of that new Canadian nationalism and determination to build something unique rests in the malaise that exists in your land . . . what appears to many as the sudden and tragic disappearance of the American Dream . . . which in some ways has turned into a nightmare.[35]

With increasing frequency during recent years Americans have been speaking to this problem. Sometimes they refer nostalgically to the America that once was—to the hopes and aspirations that once excited the world but now appear to lie in ruins. At other times they lament our lost will to work, pride, individualism, and respect for property.

"The United States was to be the admiration of the world," people say. "All the nations were to come to us to see how we did it. What happened?" All too many reports come to us about how hated and feared we are in the lesser-developed nations. We are called "ugly Americans," and signs greet us with slogans such as "Yankee, go home!"

President Richard M. Nixon expressed similar concerns early in the 1970's. In speech after speech he lamented that the "apostles of defeatism and self-doubt" were undermining the moral strength of America. He feared that, while we could not be best in every single area, we were resigning ourselves too often to being second best in the world. "Once a nation ceases trying to be number one," he warned, "that nation will not be a great nation. Let it not happen to America."

Has the American Dream indeed become a nightmare? I believe that such pessimism is nonsense. It shows a tragic lack of understanding of the nature of life and dreams. The American Dream is still the dream that it was. Its fulfillment and accomplishment still rest in the future, though we have come a long way down the road to its achievement. But it is not a static thing. Here is where some of the misunderstanding lies. It is an aspiration that continues to grow with its achievement. As we have achieved, we have become discontented with the gains to date. Were we not discontented, there would be no possibility for further growth and realization of an ever-expanding hope for our people and others in the world.

In offering this viewpoint I am not unaware of our failures. Let me describe some of them briefly as background for an interpretation of the more mature, creative American Dream that I see emerging. There is no need to be romantic, to overlook our difficulties and distresses, or to be apologetic for our efforts to date.

First, we no longer stand with open arms to the peoples of other countries. This is the nation that once inscribed on the pedestal of the majestic Statue of Liberty the stirring lines of Emma Lazarus:

> Give me your tired, your poor,
> Your huddled masses yearning to breathe free,
> The wretched refuse of your teeming shore,
> Send these, the homeless, tempest-tossed, to me:
> I lift my lamp beside the golden door.

For some years that lamp has been greatly dimmed. We have imposed restrictions on immigration. In fact, we have restricted entry of our closest and best national friends abroad. During World War II we were not able even to open the door to the persecuted Jews of Nazi Germany, to our shame and that of all civilized peoples.

Second, the American environment is no longer what it used to be. Once a wilderness, a frontier land of perpetual beauty, wonder, and natural resources, this country is now clogged with cities, its countryside a favorite dumping ground for refuse and overflow. Many of us still carry in our minds a picture of sheep lying dead in 1971 on a beautiful Western plain, casualties of leaking poison gas from a military facility. Once magnificently beautiful Lake Tahoe is polluted; so are lakes Erie, Ontario, Michigan, Winnipesaukee, and numerous others. We dare not eat fish caught in the St. Clair River (Detroit) and other rivers.

Third, something has been happening to the individualism and independence of which we were once so proud. The frontier man needed nobody's aid, charity, or benevolence; at an early age people in all walks of life learned to earn their own way. Now we are covered by Social Security, old-age benefits, Medicare, Medicaid, group pension plans, and other guarantees of assistance. There is virtually no industry in the country that is not protected directly or indirectly by tariffs, subsidies, or quotas. Unions protect their membership against many applicants for admission. Companies conspire to insulate themselves from competition, despite paying lip service to the antitrust laws. One could go on at some length with similar examples.

To compound the disillusionment thus created in many people, some foreign critics see violence in America as an outgrowth of the brand of individualism that we were proud of. The "quick gun" of the old West is seen as the root of the violence in our cities.

Fourth, the quality of our freedom seems to have deteriorated. The traditional American could be his own man. He could think as he wanted to think. Now, increasingly, we are putting up with restrictions on our freedom of speech. Many of us are afraid to speak our minds on important occasions. Suppression and repression grow. Athletic coaches, businessmen, educators, and other officials try to make young people conform to certain norms of dress and grooming. (I remember an athletic coach in Michigan telling the press with much pride that none of his hockey players had the *right* to wear long hair or long sideburns!)

My friend Harry Essrig, formerly minister at Temple Emmanuel in Grand Rapids and now a Jewish leader in Los Angeles, once told me that several students at Pacific Palisades High School came to him, after being turned down by other groups in the city, and asked permission to have Angela Davis speak to them in his synagogue (this was while Miss Davis still taught philosophy at the University of California, Los Angeles). Essrig agreed, she spoke to several hundred young people who attended, there was no violence (and practically no policemen around), and the evening was, in Essrig's words, "beautiful." But afterward adults in his congregation spoke out and some resigned. I have had a similar experience at the Fountain Street Church in Grand Rapids. When we invited Stokely Carmichael to speak to us several years ago, considerable flak and hostility showered on us from other parts of the city. Some people are still cold to me as a result of that time. So much hostility merely because we allowed an unpopular person to *speak*.

As I write this, I know of at least three groups that are seeking Constitutional amendments restricting the U.S. Bill of Rights. Who are they? Flag-waving conservatives. I do not hear Americans sounding as if they were much concerned about the three groups. Yet if the action were coming instead from the so-called liberals or radicals, surely there would be a tremendous uproar. Activities and reactions of this kind constitute a grave threat to our freedom.

Fifth, this nation has long been famed as a land of equality. Is it really? Not many Mexicans think so, or Indians, or blacks. It is not at all clear that we really want equality of opportunity.

Sixth, our revered concept of equal justice for all is under a cloud. If the statistics we read in the newspapers and magazines are near-correct, the justice a person gets in our court system depends in large degree upon his finances, social status, and political strength. The consideration that a murderer from a well-to-do family is likely to get is of a much higher quality than that for a poor or undistinguished person.

Seventh, this nation recently lost a war. How many of us learned with pride, during our youth, that the United States had never been defeated by another nation? How many patriotic Americans found the prospect of withdrawing from Vietnam almost unbearable because of this long tradition of winning?

Eighth, the United States traditionally has been a religious, God-fearing nation. We were to be the religious hope of the world. Now our churches are emptying. There is far less confidence than there used to be in a divine, transcendent God. The motto on our coins, "In God We Trust," has become meaningless to a large part of the population.

From Youth to Maturity

These eight shortcomings of the Dream are serious; they show that it is vulnerable and subject to criticism—and it should be criticized. But that does not mean that the Dream has become a nightmare. In our everyday experience, are the dreams of adolescence ever realized in maturity in the same form that they were held in adolescence? I refer not to the fact that a person's dreams may become less ambitious because of his complacency or loss of self-confidence, but to the fact that dreams naturally become more realistic and understanding as one matures. The same process has happened to our dream as a nation. We had an adolescent dream, and it was beautiful. Now our dream has changed as Americans have grown in experience and awareness of the world, but it is still beautiful.

Every girl or boy who has grown into womanhood or man-hood knows that there are major differences in the adult world from the world of youthful aspiration. For instance, that gangly youth whom people smiled at and encouraged, who felt he had the world in his grasp and knew exactly what should be done (and that he could do it!), comes to find that it is a different story when he becomes a man among equal men. No longer is there that benign tolerance of youthful aspiration. Now in competition at almost every step, he finds that what looked so easy is not really easy. He finds that those visions he once entertained somehow or other have become different.

Does this mean that he has lost his ideals? Of course not. The new experiences make a creative difference in the way he sees, feels, and thinks. He discovers that responsibility transforms the way he wants to behave. He comes to understand virtues and necessities that he had not comprehended at earlier ages. He appreciates new values, such as these:

Patience may mean more than *strength*.

Understanding may mean more than *courage*.

Wisdom may be more important than *technical knowledge*.

Cooperation and participation in the community, painful as they are, may be more important than the *arrogant independence of youth*.

With changes of this nature in his thinking, his dreams and ideals necessarily change too. But they do not become nightmares! What has happened in the case of the youth who has become a man is very much like what has happened to a young nation that has become mature.

To illustrate our transition as a nation, let me offer two illustrations. Although they represent clashing viewpoints, they were close together in time and came from close friends and associates. This suggests the turbulence and internal stress of maturation—the intimacy of old and new, of change and resistance to change, of learning and nonlearning. A nation does not grow up in neat, logical stages, nor does its dream mature painlessly.

During the mid-1950's, Secretary of State John Foster Dulles articulated the adolescent dream of America. Speaking and writing often on his global travels, this powerful, able, and strange man urged Americans to recapture the crusading spirit of the early days of the Republic, to rekindle the conviction of those days that this country had something better than anyone else, and to carry their beliefs around the world. He wrote:

> Those who found the good way of life had a duty to help others to find the same way. . . . Our foreign policy is not just a United States foreign policy; it becomes the foreign policy of many peoples.[36]

Could there be a better illustration of a youthful dream? Is there any area—one's home, one's circle of friends, or society, not to speak of the world—where one is justified in assuming that he has not only what everyone else wants but also what they need?

My second illustration comes from Dulles' chief, President Dwight D. Eisenhower. Here was a man who knew the meaning of power. After possessing and wielding unprecedented military power, he became the political leader of the United States, in which capacity he learned that he could not operate as a military commander operates. In November, 1954, after the Korean War, the Chinese announced that they were going to sentence thirteen U.S. airmen as spies, contrary to all our agreements and understandings, and contrary to accepted practices in warfare. (Some of those airmen were only recently released.) Americans responded with anger. Many wanted to blockade the coast of Communist China, others called for an invasion of China, some demanded nuclear retaliation to "teach them a lesson." Who were we, the leading power in the world, to stand by and be insulted by an unrecognized power? But President Eisenhower was not swept up in the storm of emotion. He said:

> A president experiences exactly the same resentment, the same anger, the same kind of frustration when things like this occur as other Americans; and his impulse is to lash out. . . . In many ways, the easiest course for a president and for his administration is to adopt a truculent, publicly bold, almost insulting attitude. . . . The sensible path, the hard way, is to have the *courage* to be patient—tirelessly to seek out every single avenue open to us—in the hope of *leading* the other side to a little better understanding of the honesty of our intentions.[37]

This statement, reflecting experience, realism, and understanding of relationships, is an expression of a more mature American Dream. No adolescent illusion here that our country will brook no nonsense from other countries! No naïve notion that our way is right and that if other nations do not know it, they will learn soon because we will enforce it on them! This is the statement of a man and a growing sector of his people who knew that in a different world we had to dream different dreams and carry them out differently. Here was recognition of the ancient wisdom of Isaiah. They that wait upon the Lord shall mount up with wings as eagles, but if they cannot do that, they shall run and not be weary, and if they cannot do even that much, they shall at least walk and they will not faint. (Isa. 40:31.)

Some people—those who clamored to use guns on the Chinese—felt that the U.S. flag did not fly quite so proudly after Eisenhower's decision. Others felt much the same way in 1968 when we decided to begin withdrawing from Vietnam. In each case I believe that they were wrong. For one thing, they failed to appreciate the problems of national manhood and the implications of these problems for our future. Let us consider them next.

Problems Without Parallel

The United States faces problems of maturity that have been faced by no other nation in history. Unless we are aware of the singular scope and depth of these difficulties, we cannot judge the value of our achievements. We may not, in fact, be able to see that we are achieving anything at all. In many areas, the problems we face are so unusual that the American Dream cannot be understood without reference to them. No spiritual person can fail to be impressed by them, for they are written on our actions and inactions, our institutions, our environment, our moods, our faces.

For example, the unprecedented enormity and complexity of the United States today make it a totally different nation from what it was fifty years ago or even twenty years ago. No other nation combines so much size, so many numbers, so much complexity, so much diversity with such modernity of approach. No standard formulated in the past shows how to operate with these conditions. No one living or dead could tell us how to do it. It is very easy for those who are not in this position to criticize us. But until they are involved as we are, they cannot know; what they say can have no basic significance. They are like nonswimmers telling a swimmer how to improve his stroke.

But, some will ask, is our situation *really* so different? For instance, have not countries such as France and Sweden long since confronted the problems of maturity? Yes, but neither they nor any other nation in Western Europe comes close to ours in sheer numbers of people, institutions, area, output, and interrelationships. What about the Soviet Union? Its immense diversity of ethnic groups is comparable to ours, its area and population are enormous, and at least in the large urban centers there is the complexity of a modern industrialized society. However, much of the Soviet Union is still an agrarian economy—and, more important, without freedom of speech and press the Russians have no opportunity to develop the diversity, contrast, and complexity of viewpoint that have become so central to the American character. What about Communist China? Here is a nation that aggressively believes that it knows what is best for us. To support its contention, it can point to size and complexity even greater than ours when it comes to area, population, environmental contrast, and certain other features. But the problems this great country faces are more akin to those we had a century ago than the ones we have now.

Again, the United States is the only nation in which scientific attitudes are characteristic of most of the people and in which scientific resources are prolific in every region. Our greatest scientists are confused over what to do with their skills; our educators are at odds with one another as to the role of technology in the curriculum and instruction; scientific methods are debated not alone by such as physicists and biologists but also by market researchers, public opinion analysts, athletic trainers, nutritionists, and countless other groups. It is fair to say that our whole nation is uncertain, confused, and anxious about the role of science and technology in our life, from questions of goals to questions of involvement.

As any newspaper reader knows, our struggles with such issues are intense and, it would seem, fraught with mistakes. But we are not giving up. We are determined to find ways through the problems.

Affluence is also an unprecedented problem. No nation in the world knows the affluence of the United States today. Our laboring class has become the middle class; the middle class, an upper class. The temptations, sicknesses, faults, failures, and opportunities of such affluence have no precedent in the world. The few other nations that may come close to us in degree of affluence do not have the power, size, and complexity of the United States.

We do not know yet how to use this wealth. Although our young people are surely on target with many of their criticisms, we are far from sure about the precise nature and seriousness of the difficulties of affluence. But we are bent upon learning how to understand and live with the condition, and the knowledge we gain may be a light to other nations when they reach a similar state.

Then there is the problem of power. The United States possesses military and economic power that no other nation except the Soviet Union possesses or ever possessed. In our adolescence as a people, we saw power as a solution to our problems, and we worked mightily to acquire it. But now that we possess it, we find that it is not a solution but a creator of more problems, and on more than one occasion controversies over the use of our power have caused dangerous schisms in public opinion.

How are we to handle our enormous power in this complicated world? We know now that we cannot send our gunboats out to some trouble spot and quell the forces that offend us. We must do the job in some other way, and we are not sure what way. Savants in other nations may criticize us and derogate, but they are in no position to shed light on our problem. Have they stood where we stand? Do they know what it is to have power and to be called upon, regardless of one's desires, to do something?

We cannot stand aloof from any serious problem overseas. We are subject to demands from all corners of the world. The United States did not want to get embroiled in Korea in 1951 —the record is clear about that—but we did not know how to stay out. Because of our power we were also sucked into the Vietnamese conflict, with all its ugly features and consequences. In hindsight we can see how we might have stayed out, but at the time it was far from clear to us how to manage noninvolvement—and it is far from clear how we will do that in future emergencies. Every nation in desperate straits appeals to us. It is of no use to pretend that we can turn our backs on them; that would be like someone with money trying to pretend he does not have it so that fund raisers will not bother him.

Many knowledgeable and articulate people darkly prophesy that our power will kill us, that we will take our turn with the Romans, Spanish, French, and others. Yet we are struggling to learn how to live with it, and we are learning. If we succeed in finding the right role for power, it could indeed become an asset, as strong leaders have hoped it would all down through history. But its value and utility will be different from what they envisaged.

Guidelines for Dreamers

Now let us look ahead. How does the spiritual American try to approach the problems and opportunities of a more mature American Dream? What distinguishes his manner of thinking about the Dream from that of other people?

I shall set forth some principles of a spiritual approach. Men and women who are strong in spirit will apply them in different ways, will differ about their implications, and, it is hoped, will find better ways to state them and extend the list.

But as *principles* of action these ideas, I believe, fairly characterize the new, more mature American Dream.

1. *Society is a delicate and unbelievably complicated organism.* This is one of those propositions which seem completely obvious to an intelligent person, but we need to ponder it more, for often we do not *act* as if it were true. We need, as behavioral scientists say, to "internalize" this proposition.

The world is not for exploitation in the common sense of that term. It is not mud to be formed, plastic to be molded, manpower to be manipulated. Because of its intricately related chain reactions, there is difficulty in knowing when and how to take from the world. I am not arguing for inaction or passivity. I am arguing for a spiritual point of view: destroy nothing without careful rational and irrational regard for the cost, remembering that nothing is destroyed without a cost of some sort at some time to human life, and, more important still, that the costs may be beyond our ability to trace and evaluate. In the case of a cancerous growth, removal is done at a cost to the body, but the surgeon can be fairly confident that whatever the cost is, it is outweighed by the gain to the body. However, when we destroy a person's self-confidence, freedom, or life, there are so many subtle and nonweighable costs involved in that person's relationships with others and in our guilt as destroyers that we can never be sure how much damage we are doing.

In *Darkness at Noon*, Rubashov realizes too late, as he waits for the executioners to come to his cell, that a person is not "the quotient of one million divided by one million." Rather, a person is part of what Rubashov thinks of as an oceanic state:

> One's personality dissolved as a grain of salt in the sea; but at the same time the infinite sea seemed to be contained in the grain of salt. The grain could no longer be

localized in time and space. It was a state in which thought lost its direction and started to circle, like a compass needle at the magnetic pole; until finally it cut loose from its axis and traveled freely in space, like a bunch of light in the night.[38]

The dream of spiritual people is for a greater, more sophisticated understanding of the maze of delicate relationships that bind us together as a society—a society in which each person is but a "grain of salt," yet where the infiniteness of society is contained in the "grain of salt." It is not enough to seek this understanding in a factual, logical, analytical way alone—the social organism cannot possibly be comprehended on computer printouts or logic diagrams. It is essential to pursue the understanding with mind *and feeling*. Rubashov's understanding, for example, came through the pores of his body as well as his intellect, and is expressed by Koestler in such terms.

2. *Rightness is fickle.* The rightness of a cause may change when we begin fighting for it. We may destroy the good we intended to do by using our "clout" to get our way. If a well-intentioned society could right the wrongs it sees simply by forcing its will on a situation, Americans and other peoples of the world would not have stumbled nearly so often as they have all through the centuries.

For proud and intellectual people, this guideline is humbling and frustrating. Its validity is due to the nearly incredible delicacy of relationships in an organic world, as just described. To achieve any objective in that tangled network of interdependence is to upset the balance—sometimes in inexpensive ways, sometimes in expensive ways. In addition, people of great sincerity, conviction, and energy tend, in their enthusiasm, to justify questionable means by the noble ends sought. Yet in the final accounting of a movement, it may well be that the means employed are more significant than the objectives sought, for while objectives are only notions, measures and means are in the "here and now," and hence have unavoidable consequences.

The implications? Our approach to the problems of size and complexity is an example. No matter how clearly we see a solution that is right, it will not remain good enough once we try to bulldoze it through at the expense of democratic procedures, the rights of small opposing groups, or the credibility of leaders with followers. For instance, a determination to maintain law and order at the cost, if necessary, of a fair trial to a few violators may be a hollow achievement when, though the streets and parks may be made safe to walk in at night, public disillusionment with the judicial system sets in. Again, the victory of a minority or feminist group may become meaningless if equal opportunity in an organization is won by playing other employee groups off against themselves and destroying working relationships important to the future life and viability of the organization.

3. *The world does not respond to power.* Late in 1962 President John F. Kennedy held a television interview with three newspaper reporters. In response to a question, he said he found his job more difficult than he had thought it would be. The problems were harder to cope with than he had expected, and one of his greatest surprises was the discovery that, in spite of the enormous strength of the United States, it could not achieve what it wanted.

I found this a simple but penetrating observation, especially since it came from a young man who was not unacquainted with power when he came to the Presidency, who had grown up in a wealthy family and had known from infancy what economic and social power was, and had learned in World War II what military power was. In spite of all this experience he was finding out that the most powerful nation on earth could not achieve what it believed should be achieved. There was an implication that the country would not be able to do what it believed right and necessary even if it had ten times as much power. In 1962 examples such as the Bay of Pigs fiasco in Cuba, the Congo, and Laos could be given. Since then numerous other illustrations could be added, including, of course, Vietnam.

Most of us, when we were young, told ourselves that when we grew up, we were going to "set things straight." One cause of bitterness in youth today is its impression that national and local leaders are not using their power to right the wrongs of society and the world. How differently they would manage their families, young people tell themselves, if they were the parents! What a job they would do in business, if they were in top management! If only they were in public office, what they wouldn't do to solve the problems of the city, state, and federal governments! They are disillusioned with us elders because we have used our powers so weakly.

Now, there is no doubt that we elders have reneged on many of our responsibilities, made many poor decisions, and become too frightened to do numerous jobs that should have been done. Still, there is great naïveté in youth's belief that far greater achievements could have been made simply out of desire. President Kennedy's observation is pertinent: when a person or a generation grows up and acquires most or all the power it had imagined it would, it still will not be able to achieve efficiently the great goals it sets for itself. This may be cause for dismay for some—and certainly it is not a theme that luncheon club speakers or speakers at graduation would enjoy propounding. But it is a truth which all people should learn as early in life as possible, and which the powerful U.S. nation should understand and apply in decision-making. There is an enormous gulf between what we believe with all our hearts should be done and what can be done.

This guideline, too, has important implications for this nation's approach to its great problems and for the American Dream. We must put away adolescent expectations concerning the value of great military, police, economic, and political power. We must not count on power to help with more than a few limited (though important) tasks, such as deterring would-be aggressors or curbing the rule of organized crime. Nor must we invest too much energy in creating force, for a law of diminishing returns is applicable, and, like the wise "portfolio investor," we need to diversify our expenditures.

Norman Cousins saw the point when he wrote an editorial criticizing a Presidential decision to commit U.S. fighting forces to Cambodia in 1970. As mentioned earlier, the White House justified the decision on the grounds that Americans had to demonstrate their "manhood." Cousins wrote:

> The trouble with the manhood game is that it is played at the expense of man. The inevitable result of a competitive display of national manhood is to create the stage and the occasion for an ultimate assault on human life.
>
> There is a wider, positive definition of manhood that takes in more than just raw force and the will to use it. Manhood has something to do with maturity, the comprehension born of experience, and the capacity for making moral judgments.[39]

4. *Strength breeds weakness.* Just as the mighty dinosaurs crashing through the forests probably never saw cowering in the shadows the smaller creatures that were to outlive them (including man's ancestors), so the great strength of a person, family, company, or government may make it oblivious to the small voices of warning or opposition. For instance, economic

authorities point out that warning signs of consumerism were apparent long before many corporate giants suddenly found themselves caught in murderous opposition from consumerists such as Ralph Nader and aroused government regulatory agencies. The great strength of these corporations made it unnecessary for them to listen to the opposition when it was weak, with the result that they did not make the minor revisions that could have averted major and costly consumer battles later on.

Examples such as the foregoing are only the more obvious ones, and there is a far more important limitation of strength: *it does not work on the spirit.* In fact, it may corrode the spirit. Military, political, economic, organizational, and social strengths are all ineffective in reaching the spirit of a person or a group, because spirituality exists on an entirely different dimension from force. The great leaders of Christianity and of some other religions who said that force may be used to destroy the body but not the spirit were not talking mysticism; they were expressing a truth that has been "laboratory tested" in countless numbers of circumstances and times: a person is greater than the power structure.

We may force or buy a person's obedience, but we cannot make him love and respect us. We may force a confession from a prisoner, but we cannot make him agree with us. We may use emergency authority to set up the kind of political or judicial system that we know is best for a community, but we cannot make residents support it. We may use our vast dollar reserves to buy allies or economic partners overseas, but we cannot make them feel committed to our programs. In each case our weakness is the false sense of independence and arrogance that we acquire because of our strength, whereas what reaches the spirit of another person is our acknowledgment of our dependence, our vulnerability, our relationship with him.

This guideline has many applications to the problems of

modern America. One of them is race relations. Until we in the white majorities realize our dependence upon and brotherhood with members of minority groups, we will have no real success in making those people partners in defining and achieving the American Dream. We must not let our pride in our ability to call the shots economically, politically, and socially blind us to the fact that a sense of awe and humility, and a willingness to be hurt and to be changed, is what is most needed from us.

5. *Victories of the spirit are nonquantitative and noncompetitive.* Spirituality, as explained in Chapter 4, is a sense of relatedness. It is the capacity of a man or a woman to combine mind and body (or thought and feeling) in the effort to see connections, establish relationships, and find, beginning at one point in the web of life, how his or her whole life is supported by the life around. Starting in one place, a person follows on and on until he senses that it all has to do with him, and he with it. *Any* time in a person's life that he sees relatedness, he will find meaning, strength, quality, value.

Therefore, spiritual victories are always warming, because they are supportive and dignifying; and their warmth is always enduring, because they bring an understanding that grows. In contrast, a quantitative triumph does not do these things. It may bring comforts and satisfactions, as money and fame often do. But when a victory is quantitative, there is always more to be sought, and there is almost always somebody right behind who might take it away. So the victor cannot rest. Moreover, as the person grows older, the capacity to win quantitatively begins to fail, and he begins to live in dread of losing that capacity. This is enough to drive a strong person to distraction even in the heydays of victory. He knows he cannot keep on winning quantitatively forever.

We Americans are very victory-conscious. However, many

events that we call victories are not spiritual victories. For instance, a triumph over another person is not such a victory, because how can the spirit be joyful over the beating of another human being? There are no losers with spiritual victories, and there is no boredom. A long succession of successes in outmaneuvering another nation at the diplomatic table could not qualify as spiritual victories, for the repetition would become boring after a while.

Spiritual victories do not invite comparison. They may have to do with little everyday matters or large matters of state, but always the warming effect is the same. When a person does a difficult or unpleasant task, such as writing a letter that has bothered him or stopping to talk with a person he is embarrassed to see, that is a spiritual victory if done for the sake of a relationship. A person who quits a secure position to do something that he considers more worthwhile, despite the personal risks being taken, is winning in a spiritual way because he is motivated by the ties that bind him to the community. Parents who work to raise happy, responsible children are spiritually victorious, for their children are links between present and future as well as between the family and the community. A public official who risks reelection in order to do what he considers right for the country is a spiritual victor, for he acts out of a sense of relatedness with others. But there is no hierarchy of importance among these different types of success, no "pecking order."

All this does not mean that the spirit is indifferent to quantitative achievements, such as a rise in industrial production or a successful tariff negotiation with another nation. It does not mean that it is indifferent to events in the National Football League or a relative's effort to win an award. But it means that the spirit is sensitive to the thousands and thousands of victories that are won every day by people conscious of their sense of community and mutual dependence. It will see in *that* process the victories that are most important to him. A spiritual person will not lack for reason to celebrate and feel joyful, for he will see victories often in his own life and in that of others.

The more spiritual we become as a people, the less anxiety and concern we will feel over whether we are ahead of other nations in affluence, diplomatic triumphs, technology, or Olympic winners. We may work extremely hard and intelligently to be productive in those ways—I hope we will—but we will know that the great tests have to do with the quality of life, not the numbers.

The great violinist Yehudi Menuhin was thinking along these lines when he proposed a redefinition of some key words in our vocabulary:

> *Strength* would mean courage and support, not force and domination.
> *Work* would mean the pleasure of being of use to oneself and the community.
> *Pleasure* would mean the satisfaction of work well done.
> *Leisure* would be that state of mind and body in which both work and pleasure are seen as indivisible.
> *Love* would mean service of the highest kind.
> *Protection*, that which is offered but never imposed.
> *Discipline*, that which is summoned from inside, never from outside.
> *Progress*, that which is concerned with the widest conception of man's needs and never at his cost.
> *Freedom*, that liberty which one does not enjoy at another's expense.[40]

Toward Indestructible Greatness

In the more mature American Dream that I see forming, we will work hard and with all our scientific skills for advances in government, education, medicine, industry, and technology. However, it will not be the achievements as such that warm our hearts but the involvement and understanding that comes from seeking them. Nor will it matter if the achievements are equaled or exceeded by other peoples, or if other nations choose to follow different political ideals and economic philosophies from ours. Failure to be number one quantitatively and competitively will not turn the American Dream into a nightmare.

In a survey made by *The Wall Street Journal,* 80 percent of the respondents said that they thought the United States should lead the world in medical science, manufacturing technology, social reform, general military preparedness, and political philosophy. More than 70 percent wanted America to be first in missile defense and atomic energy; about 65 percent wanted this country to lead all nations in aerospace technology. Slightly more than half of them wanted Americans to lead in space exploration and sports.[41]

These aspirations are evidence of the energy, drive, and enthusiasm of Americans. We possess so much skill, capacity, and vigor that we are willing to set many goals and to choose priorities. But the survey suggests to me that our sights are *not high enough*—not for the modern world. Leadership in technology, power, and control is not sufficient.

I propose that we set our first and highest priority on spiritual leadership of the world. This would not be done at the expense of the other goals. Probably it would fortify them. And this would be one "race" we could not lose. If the United States were to become number one in understanding and exercise of the spirit, we would never have to worry about maintaining our lead, for every time our influence helped other nations to gain in spirituality, that gain would accrue to us too. As we saw earlier, a person cannot give his spirit away;

the more he gives, the more he gets back. The same is true of an institution or a nation.

Let me use an analogy. Down through the ages, strong men have been frustrated because they could not take hold of God, shake him, and make him do their bidding. They might gain the illusion that they had destroyed him when all they had done was destroy his work. But God is not his work; he is the spirit that creates his work. Similarly, a spiritual America is not its work—not its power, affluence, economic strength, or aerospace systems. It is creative relationships, dependencies, and involvements; it is the understanding of how to nurture the creativity that produces, among other things, material gains.

What could be the symbols of the new American Dream? There are many possibilities, and I shall suggest but a few. One could be the traditional olive branch, or the dove. Another could be festivity and celebration—gratitude for the capacities to love and laugh, for the earth and air, gratitude not diminished but enhanced by the fact that there is also much evil in the world. Another symbol might be one that peoples of the East have for the spirit—water. Water is such a fluid thing. What can we do with it? Anything we like, practically. We can make any shape out of it that we want. But water always resists us, and in the end it will be there as it was before, after we are gone with all our forms, molds, and presses.

Other good symbols could be those of our Western religious heritage, such as the child in the manger. What could be more helpless or more easily destroyed than a tiny child? Another symbol could be the man on the cross. It represents not the power of the world but man in humiliation and defeat before that power; it represents the spirit that is stronger than strength and more powerful than power, and that works through defeat and rejection. This is not the way the world thinks that things should operate, but the spirit understands that contradiction and lives with it.

The spirit does not count on victory for its nourishment. It counts on understanding, shared qualities, affection, tenderness, and love. This is why the spirit could rise triumphant from the cross. This is why, in thousands of obscure places every day, it continues to rise triumphant from the mud where it has been trampled by the boots of oppressors.

Let it be the American Dream in our maturity that we find the courage to believe in the effectiveness of tenderness and in the power of love to win, even though tanks may grind out their way, planes roar, and missiles shoot into flight. We can never fulfill ourselves through military, political, economic, or any other kind of physical strength, no matter how prodigious. We will seek to be great in spirit, and our spirit will be indestructible.

Notes

1. *The Wall Street Journal*, Sept. 23, 1969, p. 1.

2. William G. Perry, Jr., *Forms of Intellectual and Ethical Development in the College Years* (Holt, Rinehart & Winston, Inc., 1968).

3. Abraham H. Maslow, *Toward a Psychology of Being* (D. Van Nostrand Company, Inc., 1962), p. 130.

4. Joseph Campbell, *The Masks of God* (The Viking Press, Inc., 1968), p. 37.

5. Jacob Bronowski, *The Face of Violence* (George Braziller, Inc., 1955).

6. See Chad Walsh, "If You Would Know the Young, Look to Their Poets," *Think*, Nov.–Dec., 1970, p. 21.

7. Paul Simon, "Richard Cory," © 1966 Charing Cross Music.

8. John Ciardi, "An Ulcer, Gentlemen, Is an Unwritten Poem," *Canadian Business*, June, 1955, p. 36. Used by permission of the author.

9. See "The Inner Light," © Northern Songs Ltd., 1969, in *The Beatles Illustrated Lyrics*, ed. by Alan Aldridge (Delacorte Press, 1969), p. 108.

10. Walsh, *loc. cit.*

11. Hannah Green, *I Never Promised You a Rose Garden* (Holt, Rinehart & Winston, Inc., 1964), p. 96.

12. See William R. Ewald, Jr., *Environment for Man* (Indiana University Press, 1967), p. 18.

13. The most persuasive modern statement of this phenomenon is Karl Menninger's book *Man Against Himself* (Harcourt, Brace and Company, Inc., 1938).

14. Leo Rosten, *Captain Newman, M.D.* (Harper & Row, Publishers, Inc., 1961), p. 329.

15. Adam Smith, *The Money Game* (Random House, Inc., 1968), p. 300.

16. From "Choruses from 'The Rock'" by T. S. Eliot, from *Collected Poems 1909–1962*, by T. S. Eliot, copyright 1936, by Harcourt Brace Jovanovich, Inc.; copyright © 1963, 1964, by T. S. Eliot. Reprinted by permission of the publishers.

17. Vladimir Dedijer, "The Real Stalin," *The New York Times*, Nov. 28, 1970, p. 27.

18. David McClelland, *The Achieving Society* (D. Van Nostrand Company, Inc., 1961).

19. *The New York Times*, Sept. 26, 1971, p. F 7.

20. Lewis Mumford, *The Pentagon of Power* (Harcourt Brace Jovanovich, Inc., 1970), p. 173.

21. Maslow, *Toward a Psychology of Being* (Van Nostrand Reinhold Company, 2d ed., 1968).

22. See *Saturday Review*, May 30, 1970, p. 14.

23. Jane Jacobs, *The Death and Life of Great American Cities* (Random House, Inc., 1961).

24. Eda J. LeShan, "The Secret of Having Fun," *The PTA Magazine*, June, 1968.

25. For a review of these and other such volumes, see Marcia Cavell, "Visions of a New Religion," *Saturday Review*, Dec. 19, 1970, pp. 13-14 and 44.

26. *Ibid.*, p. 44.

27. Elizabeth Janeway, "Are We Making Too Much of Sex?" *Boston Sunday Globe*, Nov. 21, 1971, p. 32. Also see her book, *Man's World, Woman's Place* (William Morrow & Company, Inc., 1971).

28. The data cited are as of November, 1969.

29. Leo Davids, "North American Marriage: 1990," *The Futurist*, October, 1971, p. 190.

30. *The Christian Science Monitor*, Jan. 28, 1972, p. 10.

31. Keynote address by Donald S. MacNaughton at the Life Insurance Conference on Corporate Social Responsibility, New York, October 10, 1971.

32. See Joseph Fletcher's well-known book, *Situation Ethics* (The Westminster Press, 1966).

33. See *The New York Times Magazine*, Oct. 12, 1969, p. 144.

34. Friedrich Nietzsche, *The Portable Nietzsche*, ed. by Walter Kaufmann (The Viking Press, Inc., 1954), p. 125.

35. J. J. Greene, quoted in *The Executive*, July, 1970, p. 23.

36. Henry Pitney Van Dusen, ed., *The Spiritual Legacy of John Foster Dulles* (The Westminster Press, 1960), pp. 65, 181.

37. Dwight D. Eisenhower, quoted in *The New York Times*, Dec. 3, 1954.

38. Arthur Koestler, *Darkness at Noon*, tr. by Daphne Hardy (The Macmillan Company, 1941), p. 256.

39. Norman Cousins, "The Manhood Game," *Saturday Review*, May 30, 1970, p. 14.

40. From an address by Yehudi Menuhin to the International Music Congress, October, 1971; reported in *The New York Times*, Oct. 13, 1971. © 1971 by The New York Times Company. Reprinted by permission.

41. *The Wall Street Journal*, Nov. 16, 1971, p. 1.

Index